I FORGET...

MEMOIRS OF
JACKIE CAPORASO

Note: the background on the cover is a picture of a beautiful sunset in the Florida Keys. Michael is fishing while the bait robber is watching...

INTRODUCTION

It has been on my heart to write these memoirs for my family. I have a daughter and a son. My son has three daughters and a son. Two of my granddaughters live in Australia with their children. I have two great-granddaughters and a little great-grandson. My only grandson has been living in Japan for several years and my youngest granddaughter lives in Florida. My son and his wife live in Australia and my daughter is in New Jersey.

I am also blessed with a large extended family in the Lord. It would take too long to name them all here, but I could not have made it without them. I am also grateful to my neighbors of many years who have stood by me and helped me through dark days. All these are not only dear friends and family; they are God's angels in my life. I love them dearly. This little book is an attempt to introduce myself to all in a way that they would have never known me.

There is a classic book written by Francis Thompson entitled, "The Hound of Heaven." In poetic style, it depicts the untiring pursuit of Love after the soul who flees from God.

"I fled Him, down the nights and down the days;
I fled Him, down the arches of the years;
I fled Him down the labyrinthine ways of my own mind..."

The soul flees from God's love, but the Hound of Heaven never gives up, never tires, never falls into desperation and never runs out of hope. I am grateful for all the events in my life. I am grateful for my Heavenly Father who never deserted me. I am grateful for the many angels unawares that God placed on my way. I am grateful for each and every one who has been a part of my life and those who still are.

I am very grateful for "The Hound of Heaven" who untiringly pursues after the beloved souls in darkness... This is the story of my life…and perhaps yours.

For those whom He foreknew
He also destined from the beginning
to be molded into the image of His Son.
(Romans 8:29)

ACT ONE

France

1887-1946

VICTOR
My beloved Papa

It was on August 15th of 1887 that baby Victor was born into a loving family. At the time, Algeria was a colony of France and the family had come to Algiers from the beautiful town of Montpellier, on the Mediterranean Coast of Southern France; they had done well. They had established a business of exporting the delectable Rose Wine from Algeria. They lived comfortably near Algiers and were very happy when baby Victor came into the world. His sister Angele was just a couple of years old and now the family felt complete.

Victor grew and did well in school. As he entered his young teen years he enjoyed walking and often went by the Port of Algiers to watch the big ships load and unload their cargos. His young inquisitive mind often wondered about the far away places which these huge ships visited.

He was barely thirteen when one day he decided to walk up the ramp of one of these ships, just to satisfy some of his curiosity. He meandered to the bottom of the ship and soon found himself lost and afraid in the maze of long dark corridors. He kept walking and looking but saw no one. He was in one of the cargo bays and evidently it had been sealed and ready to go.

It seems like a very long time, but he finally found an open door and a stairway and was able to find his way upstairs. The only problem was that, now the gangway had already been pulled up and the powerful horns were blowing as the ship was slowly moving away from the shore. Victor's heart was pounding. On one hand he was very worried about his parents and family missing him, but on the other hand, he was very excited about the journey that might be ahead of him. So he decided to hide a little longer and waited until the ship was out to sea before showing himself.

This was the year 1900, and communications were not as they are today, especially in that part of the world. There were no written labor laws for children either, so when the crew discovered the lad, they did not hesitate to keep him on board and give him a job; he would have to work for his keep.

The ship was sailing toward the coasts of South America. It would go by Rio de Janeiro, Brazil and unto Argentina - a very long voyage indeed. How exciting and scary was that? The captain telegraphed the authorities in Algiers and young Victor's parents were notified of his whereabouts. All was in order for the time being.

My father smiled as he recalled the details of his adventure. How could he ever forget life aboard this ship? It was not luxurious nor was it easy and it quickly ceased to be fun. The skies were not always sunny and the sea became very turbulent at times, but the young boy learned to cope. In the end he did just fine and he became fit as a fiddle. Later, when I was set to sail to the United States from France, it was my Father who gave me good advice on how to keep from getting sea-sick by focusing on the horizon. That system works well during the day and as long as one can stay on deck looking over the railing to the horizon. My father had learned that lesson first hand.

As he recounted the story, the trip from Algiers to Rio took what seemed to be forever; it was probably months. Finally the ship docked and unloaded its cargo in the Port of Rio de Janeiro. Then it reloaded with new merchandise to take back to Algiers and that took time too. The crew was given leave to go on land and enjoy the city, but it was not so for young Victor who was confined by the captain to stay on board ship. The captain had assumed full responsibility for him and wanted to make sure he was not going anywhere.

This was one of my father's favorite stories about his youth. Is it any wonder? Yet he was not a rowdy child; my father was indeed a very mild man, but with a great sense of humor.

When Victor reached the age of twenty-one, it was expected that he learn the family business. However, he had absolutely no interest in it. By contrast, his sister Angele (I was named after her) and her husband proved to be the perfect pair to take over. And so it was, Victor left the family in Algiers to go live in France.

In the course of time my Aunt Angele and her husband had three sons. Two of them became captains in the Merchant Marines, one moved to Tunis and the other to Genoa Italy. The third, Ritou (short for Richard) became a journalist. He married an English lady and moved to England. As a reporter he made many trips to Washington DC. The Paulin family was already being scattered; that became a pattern for those who followed.

In 1954 the Algerian war for independence, a guerilla war, shattered the serenity and beauty of Algeria. It terrorized the people. Between 50,000 and 150,000 citizens were brutally murdered by mobs using extreme cruelty. The once bustling and beautiful port of Algiers was devastated. The Paulin business was ransacked and ruined and the family fled to Genoa Italy where one of their sons was situated in the Merchant Marines. Many Algerians found their way to France. The government of Algeria continued to be unstable and guerilla warfare often flared up oppressing the people and the economy. At this time, much of Algeria is recovering and developing its economy again.

LIFE IN PARIS

Victor was twenty-three years old when he moved to Paris. He enrolled in college and obtained a degree in public accounting. Then he began to work as an accountant for the largest Insurance Company in France located right by the Louvres Museum in Paris; he stayed with that company until he retired at the age of sixty. He was in his early thirties when he met the beautiful young Marcelle who became the love of his life. He fell head over heels in love with her and they married.

After seven years of marriage they conceded that they could not have children, so they set out to adopt. They found a baby boy and began the process of adoption. It seems that this was not easy to accomplish in France at the time, but they succeeded and named the baby Pierre Roger; they nicknamed him Pierrot. They were very happy.

Victor worked his way up the ranks of his Company and the family was doing well. This was in the twenties and Algiers was still a peaceful place. Then Victor's father passed away and his mother turned the importation business totally over to his sister Angele and her husband. Victor received a handsome sum of money for the part of his inheritance. With that money, he and Marcelle purchased a very nice and cozy brick house in Aulnay-Sous-Bois, a suburb to the North of Paris. By train, it was twenty minutes from Paris and the house was in short walking distance from the train station. It was ideal for Victor to commute to his office in Paris every day. It was a nice quiet place for them to raise their little boy in a pleasant suburban atmosphere. There was a large yard and they planted a good size vegetable garden as well as fruit trees and flowers. The house had its own artesian well, a wonderful source of water.

These were truly happy days, until a dreadful turn of events brought it all to an abrupt end. When the boy was barely three, Marcelle contracted typhoid. In a short time the disease had claimed her young life. Victor was devastated and now he was all alone with his little son and his nice house.

HENRIETTE CAROLINE

My devoted mother

Victor was in his late thirties. He had been married to Marcelle for eleven happy years but now he lived by himself with his little three-year old adopted son. He found a housekeeper and nanny but this arrangement could only be temporary.

One afternoon after work, it was pouring down rain as Victor left his office in Paris. He opened his large black umbrella and ran across the wide boulevard to the shelter of the awning of a sidewalk café. Many Parisians were huddled there waiting for the heavy downpour to slow down. So he closed his umbrella but as he brought it down, the sharp tip of it hit and scratched the ankle of a young woman standing next to him. Victor apologized, in French of course, *"I am so sorry; I hope I did not hurt you. May I buy you a cup of coffee or something to drink?"* The very pretty young woman was not badly hurt but she accepted the nice looking man's offer.

They sat at one of the little round tables inside the café and sipped a cup of hot strong coffee. Her name was Henriette and as "fate" would have it; her mother lived in the same little town called Aulnay-Sous-

Bois!! Henriette worked in an office in Paris and lived alone; she was twenty years old and had never been married. The rain stopped but they were absorbed in a lively conversation that ended in an invitation for the following weekend.

Henriette was very attractive and Victor worked fast. He invited her to see his house and meet his little boy; she accepted. This was the beginning of a romance that would quickly bring Victor who was now thirty-seven and Henriette who was just twenty to the altar of marriage. It was 1925 in the heart of Paris when they were married.

VICTOR

HENRIETTE

HENRIETTE MOVES IN AND MORE

It was not easy for this young woman to assume the care of a house and a little child. It was going to be a challenge; and it was. Henriette loved little Pierrot, but as the years passed by and she was nearing twenty-four, she yearned for a child of her own. She made her desire known to her husband many times but because of his age and the fact that he already had a child, Victor was set against it.

So Henriette devised a secret plan in her heart. She smiled as she recounted this to me; it was one of her fondest memories. It was in the month of May and it may well have been their wedding anniversary. She found someone to stay with little Pierrot and met her husband in Paris when he got off work.

She had rented a hotel room and brought a change of clothes for them. They could go to a good restaurant for dinner and after dinner she had made reservations at one of the famous glitzy and exciting night shows of Paris, the Folies Bergeres. It is there that the girls lift their dresses and dance the cancan. Henriette had well planned the night. At the hotel, she had ordered a chilled bottle of champagne to be ready in the room. They were not accustomed to much drinking, so the champagne went a long way and the plan worked well. I was born the following February 11th in Aulnay-Sous-Bois, exactly nine months after the well calculated escapade!

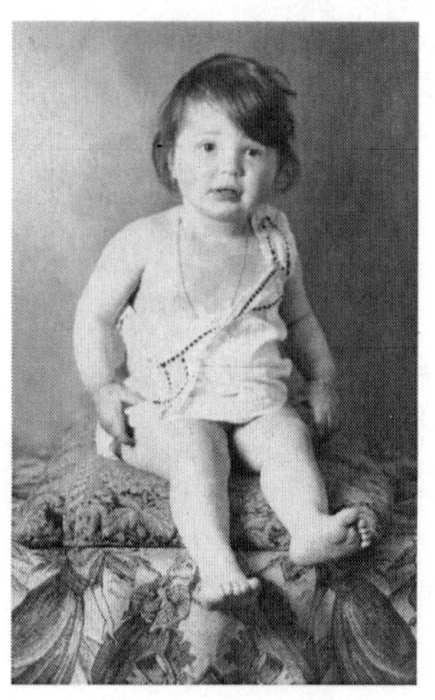

Giving a baby girl a name was a big deal in those days. So I ended up with several names and everyone was pleased! I was named Angele after my aunt. My father named me Augustine after his father August. I have the name of Leonie after my maternal grandfather Leon and of course my godfather Francois called me Francoise. My mother did not like any of these so she called me Reine saying that I was her little queen! The name Jackie came much later…

MY MEMERE AND PEPERE
(Beloved grandparents)

Henriette was a beautiful young woman. Her mother was just as beautiful and very elegant. My grandmother Caroline (I called her Memere, pronounced Memare) was born in the Eastern part of France called Lorraine on January 25th of 1882. Alsace-Lorraine is a region on the border of France and Germany. Over the years it has passed hands several times. Sometimes it belonged to Germany and sometimes to France, but the brave and sturdy people of the region never felt that they belonged to either. They felt that they were simply Alsatians!

CAROLINE FREYERMUTH

Alsace is where I find my roots on my mother's side. There was a large and close knit family in Alsace, but I did not get to know them. The only ones I knew were my cousin Eugene who built a nice house in Aulnay-Sous-Bois. He lived there with his wife Linette and son Gerard. Linette and Eugene both passed away.

Because my grandmother was raised during a time that Alsace-Lorraine was German, she had learned German in school and her family spoke German at home. Despite her lack of speaking French she left home and took steps to go find work in Paris. The family had been small farmers and Caroline wanted to do something different with her life.

Alsace-Lorraine had a reputation for excellent cooks and good housekeepers; they were very much in demand in Paris. Caroline was a good worker and an excellent gourmet cook. She went to a bureau whose purpose it is to find jobs for such skilled and reputable people. Caroline applied and quickly received a response. A very famous attorney needed a live-in cook and housekeeper; this was perfect for her.

She moved to Paris and was very meticulous at her work. The attorney who hired her appreciated her services and paid her a good wage. At the same time she was very frugal and was determined to fulfill her heart's desire and ambition. She worked and saved so she could buy her own little house in the suburbs of Paris. She dreamed of growing a large vegetable garden each year, and even having a few strawberry plants. She would plant several fruit trees and raise some chickens for fresh eggs. She would even raise a few rabbits to eat. She worked hard and set out to make her dream come true.

Caroline was only in her early twenties, but she was very disciplined. She knew what she wanted and was very serious about it. One day she heard from the family in Alsace; one of their own was coming to Paris. His name was Leon. He was an ambitious young man and would she please meet him and help him find his way around Paris. She volunteered to help him. However, not long after they met, young Leon and Caroline had fallen in love.

Leon did well too. He was not afraid to work and quickly found a job as an engineer on the French Railway System. (La Societe Nationale des Chemins de Fer Francais.) This was a job with promise of a good future. They were both very pleased. Caroline continued to work and together they set out to fulfill the dream of the house in the suburbs. So they got married in Paris and rented a small apartment; life was good for them.

When Caroline was twenty-four, she was still working and construction had begun on their little suburban house. It was not quite finished when Caroline became pregnant. On March 25th of 1905, still in Paris, she gave birth to a beautiful little baby girl. They named her Henriette Caroline.

The day finally came when Leon and Caroline moved into their new house in the suburbs of Paris. Oddly enough, by God's design, they had chosen to build in Aulnay-Sous-Bois, only it was not by the railroad station where Victor built his house, but at the opposite end of town by the barge canal that flows to the river Seine.

Caroline was very happy now. She had her little girl and her very nice vegetable garden. She was very good at taking care of things while her husband drove the mighty French trains. She had fresh eggs and chickens and even a few hutches for rabbits. She always raised a few rabbits. I remember that in the cold of winters she would get up early in the morning to make some strong black coffee for them. She fed them the warm liquid out of a teaspoon and insisted that it was very healthy for them. She knew how to take care of her rabbits and had an excellent recipe for them too!!

BAD NEWS AT THE GATE

Henriette grew up in this peaceful atmosphere. She loved her father and was very close to him. She was 13 years old now and a very intelligent and active young girl. Her mother was always busy with the house, the garden, the animals and her delicious cooking. It was the perfect family picture, but it was not meant to stay that way.

The property was fenced all around with a tall gate in front. One day when young Henriette was doing her homework and Caroline was in the garden, someone looking very official was ringing the bell at the gate. Caroline wiped her hands and face on her large apron and went to see who it might be. It was from the Gendarmerie, something had happened to Leon. He had suddenly collapsed at work and had been transported to the local hospital. However the news was not good; he had suffered a brain hemorrhage and had died instantly.

They explained to the distraught woman and terrified young girl that it all happened very quickly and that there was nothing they could have done to save him. He was just forty-two years old and his widow was thirty-eight with a thirteen year old daughter. Because of his job with the French Railroad, she received a substantial pension for the rest of her life. She also owned her house, so financially things were not bad. But he would be sorely missed, especially by his young daughter Henriette.

Caroline stayed in her house and loved it. Later she met another man, Prosper. He was an electrician who had lost his wife and son; together they became a pair. He is the only one that I knew as my grandfather; he was my Pepere (pronounced Papare) and I loved him dearly.

MY VERY EARLY YEARS

My first four years were very happy and peaceful although I barely remember them. We lived in my father's nice house in the sleepy suburb of Paris named Aulnay-Sous-Bois. My father left every morning for his office in the center of Paris, right by the Louvres Museum. He came back every evening on the seven o'clock train.

At the age of four my mother enrolled me in kindergarten and I was happy to learn to write letters and numbers and play with other children my age. It was fun drawing pictures of dogs, cats and houses with color crayons. We also took naps in school and that was very nice. My mother came to pick me up on her bicycle every day; many mothers did that. My life was very normal and filled with promise. But things were about to change drastically.

IN KINDERGARTEN

When I was barely five I clearly remember a year that was more turbulent. My father was a very gentle man and also funny and witty. I felt safe by his side but now my parents were arguing a lot. They usually waited until my adopted brother Pierrot, who was now thirteen years old, and I were in bed. They thought that I was asleep, but I was hearing their loud voices hurling angry words at each other. It disturbed me greatly. Pierre never said anything to me and I did not confide in him either.

A LIFE-CHANGING DAY

It was a cool clear morning. My father had taken the train to go to his office in Paris. Pierrot was ready for school but there was something somberly different in the house. It had to do with the way my mother was rushing around. Little did I know that on this day my life would be shattered into a million pieces; I would never be the same. My happy secure feelings would be scattered to the wind.

My mother was bringing out the several suitcases that she had packed and put away. She dressed me in my Sunday clothes and I knew I would not be going to school; it all seemed very strange and ominous.

The next thing I knew, a taxi pulled up in front of the house and the suitcases were loaded in the trunk. Then my mother walked me to the backseat of the cab and I sat slumped and fearful on the cold leather seat. I was too short to look out of the window without standing up, but when the cab drove off I stood and looked. I saw Pierrot (my brother) standing on the corner of the street with his school bag. He was weeping openly, his face drenched with tears; he did not even try to wave good-bye. He had read the note that my mother had left on the table for my father. He knew how stunned he was going to be at seven when the train brought him home.

I felt numb, without emotions, just wandering what was happening and what was ahead for me. I felt lost. My father had gone to work that morning, did he know what was happening to us? Would the painful memory of that day be engraved in my heart forever? Would I be able to continue living?

It was on that day that I began the construction of my own private, impenetrable fortress. Nothing or no one would ever hurt me like this again. I would not allow anyone to penetrate inside my heart and shatter it to pieces as this had done. And what's more if any one succeeded even a little, they would never have the pleasure of knowing it; I would never show it. (This was my thinking for a long time. Little did I know that I had a Heavenly Father and that He had planned my life from the foundation of the world).

ON A MILITARY BASE

My memory of how I arrived in the town of Draguignan on the Mediterranean Coast is somewhat hazy, but I have a few vivid memories of my days there. I know that we lived on a military base and I was surrounded by soldiers. I remember a day when someone was going to give me a ride on a horse-driven wagon. It was a large flat bed wagon with four horses harnessed and ready to pull. I was seated on the front top seat waiting for the driver to come and take up the reins. He was slow coming and for some unknown reason the horses (all four of them) became spooked and took off running.

I was just five years old and scared silly. People were running to try to catch the wagon, but it was out of control. They were shouting at the horses to stop, but they just kept running. I guess finally they stopped and all was well, but I don't remember that part very clearly. I was evidently fine, but from that day forward I was afraid of horses.

My mother was always busy working for the man who owned the canteen on base. Although it was hard for me to understand, yet somehow I knew that someday my mother and this man were going to get married. In the meantime, my mother found a nanny to take care of me; her name was Therese and I took to her like a duck to water. There was something comforting about Therese. She always smelled so nice and would put her arm around me to cuddle me; I needed that. She was my friend at first hug and she would be a huge part of my life for the next year or so.

I found out very early that there is nothing permanent in life, so there is no need to get too attached to anyone. This was a good lesson after all, as you will see later. My sojourn on the base in Draguignan was not very long. One morning, Therese and I arrived as usual to eat breakfast at the canteen. My mother usually waited for us, but that morning we were met with the news that something unexpected and very upsetting had happened. Later I learned that the nice man who owned the canteen had suffered a stroke and had died suddenly. The canteen was closed and my mother had to make some quick decisions. She had no reason or way to stay there so we moved to the nearby town of Nice, a famously beautiful town with sandy beaches right on the blue Mediterranean Sea.

Soon after, Therese escorted me to a boarding school for girls in St.Raphael. It was a very exclusive place situated on a craggy hill overlooking the Sea. There, I would be taught good manners along with regular school courses. I remember that I had to learn to be a lady and sleep with my arms outside the covers. I also remember that my hands were very chaffed and sore and they rubbed them with glycerin and put gloves on me to wear during the night; this was the remedy. The glycerin burnt and was very uncomfortable.

As beautiful as the surroundings were I really did not like the place. I not only missed my father and Pierrot, now I missed my mother and Therese too. I did not make friends there and it was a good thing because I did not stay very long. Soon, my mother came after me and took me back with her. She had leased an apartment on one of the narrow streets of Nice and she enrolled me in school. We stayed there for an entire school year.

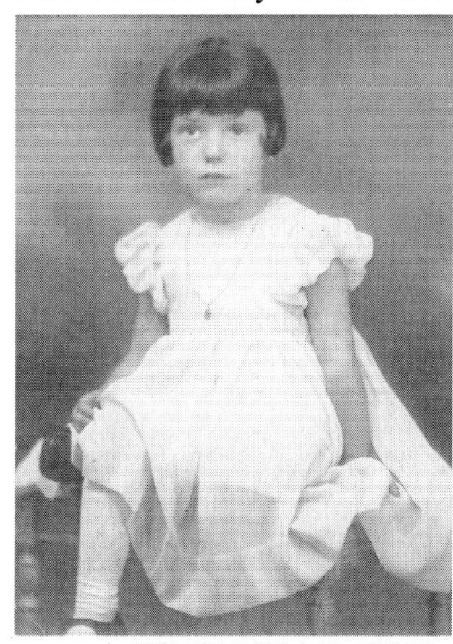

A FIVE YEAR OLD

There was a day when Therese had taken some time off and my mother decided that we would go for a ride. She had bought a car (a nice Citroen) and we were headed for Monaco. The little principality of Monaco is about

10 miles East of Nice near the Italian border. The natural scenery of the area is exceptionally beautiful. Monaco is a wealthy principality with a strip of beach on the blue Mediterranean. The palace and the casino, where most of the touristy activity takes place, are located in the town of Monte Carlo at the top of a cliff that rises vertically more than two-hundred feet above the beach. To reach the town, one must drive up a series of three roads that wind their way up by hairpin curves.

These roads are called "corniches." Their construction was one of Napoleon's grand engineering to bring tourists to the casino. A corniche (not to be confused with a cornichon which is a small pickle) is a road that is carved on the rocky side of a precipice. On one side there is a steep rocky wall and on the other there is just a thin railing to keep anyone from going over the edge. Princess Grace of Monaco lost her life in a car accident on one of these. You see many such roads in the Amalfi region of Italy where the feet of the mountains meet the edge of the sea. The very scenic Amalfi Drive near Salerno Italy is one of these beautiful drives on which Michael drove our van while I sat praying with white knuckles and sweaty palms.

So there we are, me and my mother, going for a ride and now she is maneuvering the car around the curves of these three corniches. It is getting dark when we finally reach Monte Carlo. I felt sick in my stomach from going around the many curves of the narrow road; I used to get a queasy stomach riding in cars anyway. We finally reach the top and my mother pulls into the huge parking lot of the brightly lit Casino. People are coming in and out of the place constantly in an atmosphere of anticipation. The elegant casino building is decorated with flags from every country, waving in the soft night breeze. I am glad that we finally arrived, but I am not aware that this is going to be a long night for me.

I am not sure at this point where we went to eat but I know we did and then we returned to the casino. It was late and I was tired and getting sleepy. My mother had a pillow and a blanket in the comfortable back seat and she made me lie down and go to sleep. I fell asleep and did not know when my mother slipped away but I remember waking up and looking out of the car's back window; I was still in the parking lot and I was all alone. I felt safe in the car and knew my mother was not very far; I was right. I lay back down on the seat and slept a little longer.

When I awoke this time I looked out and saw my mother coming back. She had her purse in one hand and a small suitcase in the other. When she got in the car I noticed that her name was artistically painted on the cover of the little suitcase. She saw that I was awake and gave me a kiss and brought me into the front seat. Down the hairpin curved road we went and back to our apartment in Nice. We arrived about time for breakfast and stopped on the way for a nice croissant and coffee. As a child I was always allowed a bowl of hot milk with a little black coffee in it for breakfast.

TO THE CITY OF LIGHTS

A few days later my mother had a long talk with Therese; she asked her to come to Paris with us. She needed her to help take care of me. To my delight, Therese accepted. So off we went with my mother driving her Citroen on the main road to Paris. As usual when I rode in the back seat I was car sick! We had to make several stop on the side of the road and I was having a terrible time, but with a lot of patience we made it to the City of Lights.

I cannot recall much of our first days in Paris but I know that I spent a lot of time with Therese. She had an apartment on the sixth floor and there were no elevators; we had to walk up a lot of stairs. Then the next thing that I really remember is that my mother had purchased what in Paris is called a boutique; it was a neighborhood store. It consisted of a fairly good size store front with two large display windows and an awning that was rolled back at closing. There was an efficiency apartment in the back. I found out later that my mother had bought her boutique with the contents of that little blue suitcase with her name artistically painted on the cover. She had done well that night in Monte Carlo.

From that time on, the boutique and the little efficiency in the back was our home. The place was filled with all kind of merchandise, from magazines and newspapers, to toys and school supplies. It had ladies' hosieries and men's shaving cream, a drawer full of all kinds of buttons and sewing needs; it was a veritable neighborhood dime store. My mother was very congenial and if any customer needed anything she would quickly supply them. It was not long until her little store was very popular and everyone just loved her. She was an excellent business woman with a great personality; she was a winner. My mother was a believer but she never read the Bible! At any rate she was a hard working lady and the Lord was blessing her; that was good for me too. I was glad to be in Paris because I was a lot closer to my father and my grandmother too. I knew I would get to see them more often.

DEAR LAURENCE
And my first prophetic dream

Shortly after we moved to Paris, I went to visit my grandmother and grandfather in Aulnay-Sous-Bois. I also visited my father who lived in the same lovely brick house. Pierrot was away to horticultural College in Normandy, and my father had re-married a lady named Laurence. She was extremely nice and took very good care of me. She also took me to market with her and she would let me pick out what I liked best to eat. She was an excellent cook. I really liked her a lot.

MARKET DAY WITH LAURENCE

These were the 1930s when refrigerators did not exist in private homes in France so Laurence went to market three times a week to buy fresh meat and vegetables. I admit that because of her business, my mother did not have much time for cooking, so I had become a very picky eater with a poor appetite. But Laurence's cooking was very tasty and I ate better at her house. I also ate well at Memere's house.

My father's house was the third from the corner and each evening he came home on the seven o'clock train from Paris. He walked from the railroad station and I waited for him with great anticipation. I listened for his familiar whistle and just before he reached our street corner, I heard it and darted out to meet him. I would jump up in his arms and then we walked the half a block home together hand in hand until we reached the gate with two stately trees on each side sheltering the homey red brick house. This was a nightly ritual while I was there in the summer.

There was such a bond between us, my Papa and me. It was still daylight after supper so we would often go for a walk together. He would ask me about my day and he would tell me stories about his. He had a way of making me feel good, and smart too. Sometimes we would play word games as we walked, or else we would just walk in silence. He always made me laugh with his great humor; I loved him so much.

It was during one of my visits at my father's house that I had a vivid dream that stayed with me the rest of my life. It was the only dream that I remember at that age and of course I did not say anything to anyone at the time; only I kept seeing it over and over again.

In the dream *I was standing near the railroad station in Aulnay and as I looked where the many rails come in to the station I see this huge ship. It should have been a train there but instead it was a huge boat. At the time I called it a boat because I did not know the difference but later I realized that it was actually an ocean liner.*

I had seen a few sailboats or yachts on our stay on the Riviera, but this was so different and so big. On top deck I could see colorful flags of all kinds flapping cheerfully in the breeze. Many people were milling aboard the ship. I knew that this ship had come to take me to a far away country where there were palm trees. In my mind's eye I could see the palm trees in a country with beautiful blue skies. (End of dream)

That is the dream as I remember it. It made such an impression on me that although I did not understand it, I never forgot it. It was much later when I came to Florida that it came back to my mind.

After I spent the summer between my grandmother's and my father's house, I returned to Paris where I lived with my mother in the little apartment back of the store.

THE BEGINNING OF BIG TROUBLE

I think I was about six years old in our little apartment back of the store, when in the middle of the night, I awoke in pain like I had never known before. I remember being in my mother's arms as she tried to quiet me down but the pain made me scream to the top of my voice. Then everything went black. I don't remember the ride to the hospital or much else, I just have vague recollections of the terrible pain in my head and of the many nurses dressed in white all around my bed. My head was wrapped in bandages and I hurt so much that it was painful to even move my toes. I was in a large hospital for children in Paris: "Les Enfants Malades;" I would be there for several months.

I had surgery on both ears for a double mastoid. At the time there were no antibiotics and the infection had traveled up to my brain so that they said I had a beginning of meningitis. I was hanging on to life by a thread. I remember the time they gave me a very painful spinal test, and each day they change the drains in my ears; I cried a lot.

I recall the time that they had to draw blood for a test and not a drop would come out. They took what they called "ventouses" which looked like empty light bulbs and swabbed my back with iodine. Then they made quick slashes all over my back with a razor blade. They lit some alcohol on a piece of cotton inside the glass bulbs and stuck them on top of each cut on my back. This created a suction that drew enough blood for the test.

After a long time I was transferred from the Necker's children hospital to another Paris hospital called Bicerte. This hospital is more geared toward research and new treatments. It was an adult hospital but it also had a pediatric branch. It was a last ditch effort to save my life!

One day when I was laying in my hospital bed, I could see my mother on one side, and my father and his wife Laurence on the other side looking at me. This was so unusual because although my mother visited me every day, my father had never come to the hospital (I realized later that he did not want to see her). But now they are all there. I see them as through a glass that makes them look far away. I know they are talking to me but I cannot make out their words. Then I feel my body being transported very fast through a narrow tunnel. I can see a very bright light at the end of the tunnel and I can hear as it were a choir of beautiful voices singing a song over and over again as I travel through the tunnel. I know that soon I will reach that light on the other side, but this is as far as I go, I cannot remember anything else…until I awake in a strange room.

Later I was told that I had been in a coma and they thought that it was over for me. So they had sent my mother home to get a dress for my burial. Up to that time I had been in a ward with other sick children, but now I am in a dark room by myself and I am awakening from my coma. As my eyes become accustomed to the place I see a man sitting on a chair by the wall next to the door; he is eating a sandwich. I must have stirred and moaned or talked or whatever because he quickly gets up and runs out.

Soon, nurses come rushing around me and one tells the other to quick go find the doctor. They had put me in this room because I was dying and they did not want to let other children see a child die. This was a private room that they used like a "holding" room of sorts. When my mother returns with clothes for my burial, she is stunned; instead of dying I am awake and feeling much better. The scene I had remembered with my father and mother on each side of my bed was exactly that. They had been summoned because I was in a coma and not expected to come out.

But here I am and the doctor comes rushing in. He looks at me and decides to give me some kind of shot in my head; at least this seems to be my recollection. After that I distinctly remember being hungry and asking for something to eat. I told them I would like mashed potatoes with an egg on top. Later they brought me a soup plate full of mashed potatoes swimming in butter with an egg on top. I can still see the plate; I ate it with gusto. I was weak but I was healed. I never had ear troubles again in my life. I know now that God healed me so well that my hearing has been extremely keen ever since. Someone with the type of infection and surgery that I had on both my ears should have been almost deaf.

My mother was very happy. When I was so sick, she had paid a lady to go down to the grotto of Lourdes in the South of France and bring back some of that water for my healing. My mother believed that God heard the prayer of her heart; I do too. This was truly a miracle. There may be times when we feel our parents are inadequate because of the things they do or do not, but I believe that God gives each child the right set of parents to work the work that they need to prepare their hearts for His purpose. Children are raised by the Lord through the parents that He chooses for them. Many times it is through hardships that He molds them for the calling of their lives.

After a time, I left the hospital and went home with my mother. I did not stay home very long because I was very thin and needed to go out of the city to recuperate. But it was around Christmas in 1937 and the City of Lights was very bright. My mother wanted to do something special for me. I still had my head wrapped in bandages so she put a huge blue bow around my head. She laughed and said that I looked like an Easter egg.

Then she took me to the famous Ritz Theater in one of the plush districts of Paris where they were having the premiere showing of Walt Disney's Snow White and the Seven Dwarfs. That was very big for me and I enjoyed it so much. I learned to sing Hi Ho Hi Ho, in French of course. It was a night I relived in my head many times. The next two years were going to be very long for me.

THE PREVENTORIUM

Most people have never heard of a "preventorium" but I lived in one for almost two years of my young life. Most American dictionaries do not even list the word "preventorium," but I found it in a "New Century Dictionary" which was published in 1927. It defines a "preventorium" as an institution for preventing the spread of a disease, esp. tuberculosis, as by the treatment of persons in danger of the disease.

I was almost eight years old and out of the hospital where I had been so sick and where I had spent almost nine months in bed. I was in need of fresh air and good food; the city was not the best for that. I needed special care to recuperate and to protect me from catching tuberculosis as they said that my lungs were "veiled". I never did get the disease and that may have been thanks to the good planning of my father who took me to the Pasteur institute in Paris when I was an infant. It was in 1930 that they were immunizing babies with the BCG vaccine against tuberculosis. The following year or so they stopped doing this because many babies contracted the disease from the vaccine, but those who made it were protected for life; I had won that round.

Even though I was very frail and delicate, I was clear of any disease. So I was sent to a preventorium for children, way up in the Pyrenees Mountains of South Western France where the air is clean and crisp. I was with many children and our days were full. We took long hikes and even learned to do a little mountain climbing. With plenty of good food, exercise and rest, I returned to Paris much stronger. But was I prepared for the painful episodes that I was yet to face in my young life?

THE FALSE POSITIVE

My mother was faithful to take me for regular check ups at a clinic nearby. The doctor was a French lady with a Russian name. On one of my first visits, she took me and my mother aside for a very serious talk. They had done a blood test on me and found that it came back positive for syphilis. They concluded that this had been hereditary. My mother had no choice other than to accept the diagnosis. She knew she did not have the disease so she blamed my father for it. My father denied ever having had such a thing or any member of his family having had it. Now we know that it can only be passed to a baby by the mother. My mother was clean.

There were no penicillin or antibiotics available then so the doctor ordered several series of twelve painful shots. Once a week I would take the subway to a nurse's apartment and she would administer the shot. When one series was over, I would get a couple of weeks off and then begin another series. This went on for almost a year. At the end of the year, my doctor suddenly died of cancer; she was replaced by another doctor. I went in for my check up and a new blood test. It was perfectly clear and my case was dismissed. They never admitted it, but we found out later that the specific test they gave me has a high rate of inaccuracy. Today, they use a different test altogether. At any rate, this little episode kept me in Paris close to my family.

Because my lungs were still weak, it was decided that I would spend one more year in a Preventorium. This time I was sent to the beautiful town of Hendaye located where the Atlantic Ocean meets the Pyrenees Mountains on the border of France and Spain.

Hendaye is on the French side of the Basque country; one of the nicest places on earth. The many buildings of this large preventorium were sprawled out along the beautiful beaches of the town. Several hundred children from the cities lived and thrived there under the care of nurses and doctors. The days were well planned and organized and the majority of our time was spent on the beautiful sandy beach where we made sand castles, played games, did gymnastics and swam a little in the Atlantic. Sometimes we took lunch with us and went hiking on long walks. I became very tan and muscular and I felt well. We had some schooling in that place too but not as much as we would have had normally. I loved to read and spent much times with my nose in books on the beach.

I was slated to stay an entire year in Hendaye but in December of 1939, just a couple of months before my release, my mother came and asked to take me back to Paris. They were not happy to let me go early but she insisted. World War II had begun in Europe and she did not want to leave me so far from her with the chance of my not being able to get back.

THE FRENCH EXODUS

It was 1940 and I was ten years old. I was back in Paris with my mother and the German Army was marching on the City of Lights. The French Government no longer had its headquarters in Paris. It had temporarily moved the capital to the town of Vichy in Southern France. Marechal Petain was now President and he made the wise decision to save Paris by declaring it "OPEN CITY." So one day I saw signs pasted all over on billboards and buildings saying that "Marechal Petain had declared Paris OPEN CITY." I was not really sure what that meant, but I found out later that it meant Paris would not defend itself. The city was opened for the German troops to just walk in and they were on their way.

Most of the population of Paris was already gone. They had left in a mass exodus on the roads heading south. They all thought that there was going to be a terrible battle in Paris and they left all behind to save themselves. As it turned out it was much the opposite. My father and his wife had left. My mother had tried three times to put me on a train evacuating children to the South. She took me to the Railroad Station in Paris each time. A large white card with my name and information was pinned on my coat and I had a little suitcase with a few of my things; I was numb with fear. Everybody was pushing and shoving trying to get their children onto the train. This happened three different times, but each time the train became full and pulled away from the station and my mother and I returned home.

Finally, in the frenzy of it all, my mother loaded up my bicycle with things for the road. I asked her where we were going and she looked at me and said "I just don't know!" At that point it seems that strength and wisdom took hold of me and I looked at her and plainly told her, "Then we are not going anywhere. We are staying right here." And so it was that we stayed.

My mother's shop was closed now as were all the stores in Paris. There was nothing to eat and all that remained after a few days in our apartment was a can of sugar and a can of cocoa mix. When I got hungry I ate some of that by the teaspoon full, just dry. It tasted rather good—very sweet!

There were just a few tenants left in our large building. We now lived a few blocks from the store in a nice fourth floor apartment. The little room in the back of the store was not adequate for my health. We could not open the store and so we just waited. But the morning came when we opened our windows and heard someone down in the court call out, "They are here!!" This meant that the German armies had arrived in Paris.

My mother and I ran down the stairs and across the courtyard. We stuck our heads out the heavy large, ornate double doors of the building and looked toward the avenue which ran by our street about a block away. We could hear the noise of boots marching and we could smell the strange odor of the troops.

Then we saw them. Some were slowly riding in open trucks while others were marching dressed in their green uniforms. Some of the trucks were pulling cannons while others pulled mobile kitchens with pots steaming with food. This was a very painful moment in French history and my mother and I were front row witnesses. Perhaps it should have been scary, but I was not afraid, just wondering what would happen in the future.

GROWING UP DURING THE GERMAN OCCUPATION

Soon after this, Paris took on an air of normalcy. Although things were far from the same, life went on. The people who had left in the exodus slowly returned but many were killed or died on the roads; some were shot down by German planes dropping bombs on their route, others died of just plain exhaustion or hunger.

My mother re-opened her shop and even though she did not sell food, the merchandise was hard to obtain. There were no more deliveries so on many mornings my mother had to get up at four or before, catch the subway and go pick up a load of toilet soap or such things as her customers needed. It was heavy work and very hard on this brave woman who was keeping her little shop open and raising a child by herself. I know that she often regretted having left my father, but it was too late.

Life was difficult for all the people in Paris, but especially for the old and the lame. I was twelve years old and my food rations were a little better because of my age. Also my mother had a gentleman friend who worked for a coffee house. He delivered coffee and sugar to restaurants and he could exchange coffee and sugar for meat and other foods; he supplied us too.

My father and his wife Laurence had sold the house in the suburbs and now owned an apartment in Paris. They were among the less fortunate for food rations and Laurence stood in long endless lines to receive a very small ration of cheese or meat once a month. The market had few vegetables and I remember how Laurence could cook rutabagas in so many ways so that they were somewhat appetizing and tasty.

During the five years of German occupation many old people died of starvation. Winters can be very cold and damp in Paris, and the apartments were not heated during the war; it was difficult to stay warm. My mother had a little wood stove that she hooked up to the fire place. We would wet and wad up the newspapers that she did not sell that day and when they dried out they burned nicely and warmed up our small apartment. We had moved from our roomy fourth floor apartment to a smaller one on the main floor. At night we had to be sure and pull the heavy drapes over the windows, because the police came by and whistled if they saw even a flicker of light around our windows. Most of the air raids took place during the night and the once City of Lights was now totally dark.

There were many air raids, night and day, and when the sirens went off everyone was expected to run to their shelters in the basements. At school it was the rule, everyone had to go down the caves, or basements, and sit there until the all-clear sirens sounded. We quickly learned the difference between the sound of the sirens that warned of the planes coming to bomb and the sirens that sounded the “all clear”. Sometimes we would spend hours in the dark dank basements.

That was at school, but when the sirens went off and we were home, I told my mother that I wanted to stay in bed. For some reason or other my mother agreed with me and we never went to the cave at night time; we often just slept right through.

Once, I slept over at my father’s apartment and the sirens went off during the night. My father and his wife insisted that we go down. They lived on the seventh floor and of course during the war the elevators were not working. So we went down and back up an hour or so later. It was hard climbing all these steps in the middle of the night. It was hardest on old people and babies.

THE STAR OF DAVID IN YELLOW

Although life was difficult for all the citizens of France during the German occupation, it was even worse if you were a Jew. Jews were required to sew a yellow Star of David with the black letters "Juif" in the center on all their coat sleeves. They could never venture outside without it. If you were Jewish you had a curfew and must not be out on the streets after a certain hour. I am not sure what that was but I know it was early evening.

The green uniform German Army consisted mainly of very young soldiers who never made advances on any girl or woman and never seemed to bother anyone. But the ones who wore the black uniforms were more mature men and much more dangerous; they were part of Hitler's private army known as the SS or Nazis. They were not seen in the subway and very seldom on the streets but once in a while they would conduct raids on people especially Jews. Perhaps a German soldier had been ambushed and killed by some Frenchman the night before, so they were rounding up hostages to avenge that.

I remember one day when I was walking home. I had just come out of the subway station on this large plaza with many avenues branching out. I was about to cross the street to enter the avenue that led to my house when I heard the strident sound of whistles. This meant "freeze." It was some of the SS rounding up people as they were walking. They were looking for Jews but were really taking anybody, even children.

There was a very large church right by the corner where I stood and I was right by one of the side doors. I ran into that church, made my way past all the pews and hurried toward one of the side altars by the statue of a saint. It was a statue of Saint Anthony of Padua. I knelt in front of it facing the foot of the statue all worn out from people touching it over the years. I implored the Saint and waited in the semi darkness of the church. I am not sure how long I waited, but when I went out all was quiet and I continued my walk home.

I found out later that many had been herded into trucks on that day.

People who were walking across the plaza to go to the theater on the other side were pulled away and taken. They first looked for those wearing the yellow star, but they also took anyone else on those days, including little children. I know now that the Lord had made the way for me that day. He had placed me right by that church door instead of crossing the avenue to go home. Looking back I realize that there were many incidents where He had protected me.

I remember the time when I was on a train coming home from a vacation. My mother had sent me for a few weeks of summer to a quiet little village South of Paris. These people had a nice place and boarded several children from the city during the summer. There were girls my own age and we had a great time.

On the way back to Paris we heard the planes following our train. I could tell that they were American planes by the sound of their engines; the motors of the British planes did not have the same drone as the American planes. Also the British did more of the night bombing (I may have this fact backwards.)

Evidently the American planes were aware that the train carried German troops and supplies as well as French civilians. The Germans were well known for doing this. They mixed civilians with their own troops for added protection. This was a very long train with a lot of people on board. We were expecting them to bomb at any moment but nothing happened. We arrived at the Railroad Station in Paris and I quickly made my way to the Subway to go home.

When I arrived, my mother was all excited. She was so happy to see me. She had just heard the news on the radio; it had been the biggest bombing of Paris ever. The entire Railroad Station and trains were blown to bits. That was the Station I had just left.

HOW GOD USED MY REBELLION TO GET MY ATTENTION

It was June of nineteen-forty-two in Paris, a very nice summery day. There was no school that day and my best friend Paulette was not home; I was a little bored and I asked my mother if I could go on a bike ride. I remember that my mother had hired a lady to come and sew some clothes for me. She had been making me a nice pink robe and wanted me to try it on before leaving on my ride. I also recall that this lady was sewing new clothes for me because my mother was sending me to a boarding school outside of Paris. I did not say anything about that but I felt a mixture of anger and sadness when I thought of leaving her and my life in Paris.

I wanted to go on a long ride on my bicycle and I am not sure of where I told my mother I would be going. I only remember that she absolutely forbid me to go through the center of Paris, especially the narrow streets filled with traffic; she even precisely named Rue des Halles.

Les Halles is a district in the center of Paris where all the produce comes into the city for distribution to shops and markets. Rue des Halles is a narrow street, and trucks are always parked by the curb loading up fruit and vegetables for their deliveries. So that street is super jammed with traffic and people. Even though I was mature for my age, it is not a very good place for a twelve year old on a bicycle. This is why my mother, for some uncanny reason made sure to tell me not to go that way. But guess what…

I had a very nice Schwinn bicycle and the brakes had just been adjusted. They were brakes that you squeeze with your hands on the handlebar and they were adjusted a little too tight for me; I had to make an effort to squeeze them hard enough to stop. The sun was shining bright on this afternoon in June and I was happily riding down the narrow street that my mother had cautioned against. Then I was following close behind a large truck when it stopped suddenly right in front of me. I squeezed and squeezed my brakes but I was not slowing down and I knew that I was going to hit the truck. So I quickly veered to go around him before it was too late.

I came around the truck still with a certain amount of speed and came face to face with a coal truck that I had not been unable to see from behind the other truck. I hit it head on…I bounced off the front fender of the truck and was thrown under the back wheel. The driver had hit the brakes and the big black tire was rolling slowly toward my right leg. It did not crush it but it took a good piece of flesh off it.

The next thing I remember I was looking at the watch on my wrist, trying to focus my eyes with blood running down my face. It was two o'clock and I was lying flat on my back on the sidewalk with the sun shining in my eyes. I could see the faces of a crowd of people all around me; my head was spinning. A nice looking policeman was leaning over me and telling me that the ambulance would soon arrive; I was badly hurt but I could not feel my body.

I remember the ride in the ambulance; I talked a lot trying to make sense of what was happening. The next thing I remember was waking up in a lot of pain in a hospital bed. My mother was there and I had been in surgery. I recall how my right thigh was itching and I wanted to scratch it. A nurse came by and looked at it; she said that I was allergic to the tetanus shot that I had been given. I also had a hole in my head, a cut under my right arm and a very serious wound on my right leg. I had no broken bones but the flesh around my knee had been ripped off to the bone.

Days went by and all I can remember is that I would wake up and feel very sleepy. The nurse would come by with a shot and I would go back to sleep. I was beginning to enjoy the kind of euphoria that I felt when I slept. Then the day came when I asked for the shot and it did not come. I was told that the shots had been morphine for the pain but now I would just be given a pill when needed. Soon I was better and began to eat and be myself again.

Time passed by very slowly in that hospital. This was not the nice children's hospital that I had once been in, instead it was one of the oldest and most famous hospitals in Paris called Hotel Dieu. It was the nearest from the scene of the accident and it was right on the Ile de la Cite in the very heart of Paris. Ile de la Cite is an island in the middle of the river Seine. The history of Paris goes back to more than two thousand years. The city started with a tribe of fishermen living on this island. A Roman settlement had found the tribe called the "Parisii." The river favored navigation and commerce and the people worked and became prosperous. In time they freed themselves from the Romans.

The city began to expand all around the island until it became the great city called Paris. It is on this island that Notre Dame Cathedral is located, as well as the Palais de Justice and the seat of the French government. The hospital Hotel Dieu is also on this island and from my bed I could hear the bells of Notre Dame ringing the hours.

The nurses were all very nice to me, but it was war time in Paris and the drugs and the doctors were scarce. I found out that the young doctor who had performed the surgery on my leg had been straight out of medical school. Because this was his first surgery of the kind he did all he could to save my leg which was almost completely severed at the knee.

It was not painful now but I could not walk and they never let me get out of bed. They really did not have enough help and they had to give minimum care to each one. I was only twelve years old, but I was in a hospital ward with adult women, some very sick and a few even died. I stayed there about four months. This was still France during the occupation.

A NUDGE FROM GOD

As time went by, the wound on my leg was not healing and now it was beginning to smell terrible. The nice young doctor that did my surgery when I first came into the hospital never came back to see me; I found out that he had been sent somewhere else. We were under German occupation and doctors were scarce as they were quickly recruited by the German army for service, so that nice young doctor who saved my leg was no longer at this hospital. A new doctor took over my case. I cannot remember what he really looked like because I only saw him once. He took one look at my leg and said that gangrene had set in. He scheduled me for amputation the next day.

That night as I lay in my bed troubled, I began to pray. It was the first time I really consciously prayed. I had uttered repetitious prayers like the Lord's prayers or Hail Mary before, but this time I just needed to have a heart talk with God; I cried my heart out. *"God, if there is a God, please answer my plea and help me! I am sorry I disobeyed my mother and now I am going to lose my leg and I am afraid."* I tossed and cried all night until I finally fell asleep.

The next morning when breakfast was brought to the others in the ward, I did not get anything. I was told that my surgery was scheduled before lunch and I was to have nothing to eat or drink. All morning I expected to see them walk in with the rolling table to take me to the operating room but it never came. And now it was noon and they were bringing lunch to the others. My surgery must be running late, that was not unusual, but soon they brought me lunch as well.

I told them that I could not eat because I was scheduled for surgery. They looked at their ticket and said no, this is for you. Soon the nurse came and explained that an emergency had called my doctor away and that I would have to be rescheduled.

The next day a new doctor came to see my leg. He was an older man and very kind looking. He looked and gave orders to the nurse. Then he came back rolling one of those little metal tables with instruments, gauze and bandages on it. He had several nurses with him and they all surrounded my bed. Then the doctor took the bandage off my leg and took a pencil like stick off the tray and began to dig trenches into the wound on my leg.

The open wound was large and raw and it reached all the way around to the back of the knee. Later I found out that this pencil was silver nitrate and the doctor was digging out the rotten flesh from the wound. There was no anesthetic available for this so the nurses around my bed were holding me down and talking to me to help me. It was painful for sure but when it was done, the doctor said, *"I think you will be able to keep your leg!"* This was the best news ever. After that I knew that there was a God and I knew that He was real and that He loved me! He had answered my heart's cry.

MY GRANDPARENTS' HOUSE

When I was finally told to get out of bed, I had to learn to walk all over again. I had been over four months in the hospital and when I left I went to stay with my grandmother for a while; she and my Pepere helped nurse be back to normal. I took correspondence school again that year; I was accustomed to that.

I loved my Memere; she was everything I admired. She was tall and pretty. She was very peaceful and an excellent cook. She had a dog, a Belgian Shepherd Groenendael named Stop. He was about the size of a medium German shepherd, with a beautiful coat of long wavy black hair. He was a very playful and loving dog. He was actually my Pepere's dog and he was very protective of him.

My Memere also had a cat named Souris (Mouse). Souris was a short haired black cat with green eyes. She loved to curl up next to Stop; they had been buddies for so many years. Stop was about fifteen years old and Souris was nearing twenty. I had played with Stop many times on my visits at my grandparents'.

Once on one of my summer visits I had decided to play a trick on Stop and hide in his dog house but he quickly outsmarted me. He came and laid himself right in front of me in the dog house and when my grandmother came out looking for me she could not find me. I tried to call out to her but Stop would just push his strong furry body against me and I was stuck tightly between him and the back of the dog house. I was getting scared now and my grandmother was looking everywhere for me except in the back of Stop in the dog house. I had learned a good lesson that day; never get on Stop's territory.

But now I was not so playful myself. I came to recuperate from my accident and I needed to learn to walk well again. I was being home-schooled by correspondence and my Pepere helped me with my homework. My leg was quickly getting better and soon I was able to walk again with no limp. However I had a very significant scar all around the knee and that was going to stay with me for life. Later, a doctor suggested grafting skin to hide the scar but I had my fill of hospital life and I asked my mother to just leave things as they were; she agreed.

During the war, my Pepere who was always very fervent when it came to politics had a shortwave radio. This was against the law in France at the time so he kept it hid under a blanket and listened to the

British broadcast of the BBC in the bedroom. When he searched for the English station, there was a lot of static and noise but he put his ear close to it and listened attentively; he kept the volume very low. I found out later that it was Radio Free Europe from London. In spite of all his cautiousness, someone must have picked up the signal; they turned him in to the German authorities.

I had gone back to live in Paris with my mother, but my grandmother told us how two German soldiers came to the door and arrested my Pepere. He was taken to a prison camp North of Paris; they called it a camp for political prisoners. They released him a couple of years later because his health was failing; he had contracted a severe form of skin blisters called "black erysipelas" and he was dying.

After his death, my grandmother remained by herself in her nice little house. She did not garden much anymore but she continued to bicycle to market three times a week until she passed away in 1972; she was a week short of her 90th birthday.

Certain times I spent at my grandmother really stick to my memory. As I mentioned earlier she was born in Lorraine, the part of France that is on the border with Germany. Sometimes that region belonged to France and sometimes it belonged to Germany. My Memere grew up at a time when Alsace-Lorraine was German so when she came to Paris, she spoke a little French with a strong German accent. My mother's father who died when she was only eleven years old was from Alsace and so he was born and raised under the same circumstances. As a result they spoke German at home and my grandmother only learned enough French to get along. It was my Pepere who later patiently taught her to read and write French until she became very good at it.

One day, during the German occupation she was startled by a couple of young visitors in German uniforms. Alsace-Lorraine was again in German hands and all the young men of that region had been drafted into the German army. The two young soldiers that visited her were cousins who just dropped in to say hello. Because they were family she received them well and even took in their laundry; they paid her for that service.

But the next door neighbors who were not aware of the family ties decided that she was “collaborating” with the occupying German forces and after the war they accused her of being a traitor and turned her in to the authorities. Right after the war many French citizens were arrested as collaborators. Women were humiliated and paraded down the streets with their heads shaved; this was their punishment.

I am not sure why, but I guess because of her age and her explanation, my grandmother was spared the ordeal, but she was deeply hurt. Her husband had died because of the lack of care he received as a political prisoner in a German camp, and she was not a collaborator with anyone who was an enemy.

I loved her very much. She raised chicken and rabbits for us to eat and she would take me walking to the nearby forest where there were all kinds of plants that she picked for the rabbits to eat. On cold winter mornings she took a little saucer of black coffee for the rabbits to drink; she said it was good for them and they liked it too!

I enjoyed going on walks with her. During the occupation food was very scarce and it became very difficult to feed the animals, especially her dog and cat. There was no such thing as “dog food” or “cat food” in cans or bags as we have today. In those days she went to the butcher, bought cheap cuts of meat and bones, and made soups for them.

But as time went she could no longer feed them. So one day she went to the veterinarian and bought a little box of something. With tears all the way back home she carried the little box. In the back yard she had a large empty drum that had stood the test of time; there was a lid on it. She carefully and tearfully picked up the dog and then the cat, they were very old now and they were very thin for lack of food. She placed the contents of the little box on the bottom of the barrel and very carefully opened the little box. She placed the lid over the barrel and waited. There was not a stir or a sound of any kind.

Later she asked a young man to come and dig a hole in the backyard and she buried her loyal and docile animals there. It was a very sad and painful day in her life, but she had done the best for all concerned. They had had a very happy life and had been well cared for and loved and now they were very old and their time had come. I was not with her when she did this; she told me about it later.

A DREAM THAT SAVED MY LIFE

Although I had many dreams as a child, only a few remain vivid in my mind to this day. One of these was simple and very short, but it was so real; I believe it saved my life. At the time I was about seven years old and I was in the preventorium in the Pyrenees Mountains. The nurse had tucked me tightly into the bed so I would not get uncovered because she opened the windows wide to let the brisk night mountain air in. It could get quite chilly.

At one point during the night I dreamt that *"I had turned into a leaf of lettuce and now I see this large duck come by me. I knew he was going to eat me up and I began to fight. I fought with my fists and kicked with my legs with everything in me."* Then I awoke to find that in my sleep, I had turned myself around in the bed so that my head was at the foot of the bed with the sheets and blanket tightly wrapped around me. I was suffocating but because in the dream I was fighting the duck, in reality I was kicking and punching at the covers until they came loose and I my head was out. It was a fearful experience. Much later I realized that God had saved my life through a simple dream.

A MOST SIGNIFICANT DREAM

It was early in nineteen-forty-four that I had a vivid and unusual dream. At the time I lived with my mother in Paris. My leg was healed from the accident and although I had a very bad scar I was glad to have my leg and to be walking and running without any problem. My father and his wife Laurence lived in Paris now. The German occupation was very hard on the French population. Many old people died of hunger or lack of care.

My mother had finally sold the store because it was too hard to keep it supplied; there were no deliveries. She had to take the subway to go to the various suppliers and pick up the merchandise. She would leave at four in the morning and when she got to the suppliers she had to stand in line to get her orders. Then she had to carry the heavy loads back to her shop by subway. When she finally found a buyer she quickly sold the business.

The dream came early in 1944. It was one of those dreams that continue working on you for the entire day. *"I saw small airplanes doing all kinds of aerobatics all over the Paris sky. At one point the planes were so close that I could see the pilots. They were soldiers in uniforms that I had never seen before and they had striking blue eyes and nice looking faces. They were smiling and looked very friendly and kind."* The dream was powerful.

The following day, I was scheduled to visit my father and Laurence; I did this about once a month. I do not think that my mother was aware that I would often pack some coffee beans and sugar from her closet into a little suitcase to take to them.

During the war, my mother had a good friend who worked for a coffee supply house. Even though it was rationed, he delivered coffee and sugar to the big restaurants and cafes of Paris. He also did a lot of trading with butchers and grocers for meat or cheese. I really cannot explain how he did all this but I know that he brought some of these things to my mother as well. So when others were hungry, we were blessed with more than our rations.

I remember the time that my mother had traded some food for a pair of shoes for me. They were a pair of very pretty red leather loafers with leather soles. Leather shoes were rare in Paris at that time, most women or girls wore the clickedy-clack thick wooden soles. Songs were even written about those wooden sole shoes.

But my pretty red leather shoes squeaked as I walked and it made all the girls at school take notice. I felt so ashamed; at the end of the day, I gave them away. This did not please my mother for sure!

It was a night before I was due to visit my father that I had a dream that made a great impression on me and left me somewhat shaky. It was Sunday and I took the hour subway ride to my father's apartment. My father was not a "religious" man. For the most part, France is a "Roman Catholic" country; most churches are Catholic.

My father never went to church but he read the Bible. He had a set of the books of the Bible and he and Laurence would read a portion and discuss it together every night. He never said anything to me about it; I guess he did not want to confuse me being that my mother was sending me once a week to the nuns to study catechism. I spent a nice Sunday with them as always and at one point I told them about the dream I just had the night before. They were both amazed at what they heard and told me to keep it to myself, so I did.

JUNE 6TH, 1944

D-DAY

The airwaves were controlled by the Germans, the news was carefully selected by them. But there was an atmosphere of excitement and anticipation everywhere in Paris; it could be seen on everyone's silent face as they walked. Rumors were flying that the Americans had secretly and expertly landed on the beaches of Normandy. That was almost too good to be true but in my heart I knew that it was; somehow I knew that it was what my strange dream was all about.

Then suddenly, soldiers from an Army calling itself Free French were popping up everywhere in Paris. Most of the civilian population had never heard about them. They had been underground all along, under the command of General DeGaulle and General LeClerc. Rather than wait for the American troops to come nearer and liberate Paris, they had made plans to do that job themselves and make the way for the Americans to enter the city triumphant.

When the Free French showed up, the streets of Paris became a combat zone and it was no longer safe to go out; all the stores closed their doors. Almost all the Germans were taken by surprise and fled, but some stayed in hiding, trying to keep a hold on the city. It was a week of fierce and bloody combat between them and the Free French Army. The Paris subway was closed too and later they found that the Germans had wired the tunnels in order to blow up Paris before leaving. This had been the desperate plan of the Germans as the American armies approached, so the surprised attack of the French saved the city and us again.

These were exciting days. We found out that one of the French fighters was a neighbor in our own building. Each night he came to his kitchen window and gave us the news of the day; the Germans were really resisting and the fighting was intense. There was no other source of news. Food was again very scarce as the bakeries and groceries stores were all closed. Our new found neighbor friend had connections. He brought us the various fruit that he found that day. Looking back I know that it was the Lord who was looking after us, yet we did not really acknowledge Him.

I do not recall how long it took for the fighting to stop but one day we learned that it was over. The subway and all transportation were still closed but little by little the stores began to re-open. We were told to be on guard because "snipers" that had stayed behind were hiding in top floor apartments of some buildings. These snipers were German soldiers who were holed up, perhaps in some friend's apartment or their own. They still had guns and ammunition, so from time to time they shot at people walking in the streets; that was a dangerous situation.

A few more days passed and we heard that the Americans were almost at the gates of Paris. My mother and I lived not far from one of the gates of Paris so we dressed in our best clothes and put flowers in our hair to go and welcome the troops. It was jubilation like I had never seen before or since. It was the happiest day of our lives—the war was over for us. There would no longer be air-raids, no more spending time in the caves during school hours, no more shrilling sirens warning us to take cover, no more carrying the dark green metal box containing the gas mask. So many things would no longer plague us. This was truly reason for rejoicing; it was genuine euphoria.

THE AMERICANS IN PARIS

August 25th, 1944

All of Paris was lined up along the streets while tired but handsome and happy young American GIs rolled in with their tanks and opened trucks. They were very friendly, dressed in their khaki uniforms standing or sitting proudly with big grins on their faces. Most of them bent down from their trucks to shake hands with the welcoming crowds or stretch out their faces so the girls and the women with flowers in their hair and flags in their hands could grab them, hug them and kiss them.

Suddenly the cheerfulness was interrupted by gun shots ringing in the air. Snipers. For some reason, they were shooting at the people and not at the troops. Everyone scrambled every which way. The shots came from the top window of a building directly across the street from us. Because the street had been barricaded during the previous days of fighting, barbed wires had been rolled up on the sidewalk right in front of us.

An old man was standing right by me when the shooting began. I did not try to think, I just pushed him down and my mother pushed me down and we all three landed in the barbed wires while the shot just whistled over our heads. We had been narrowly missed. My pretty white organdy blouse was ripped but that did not matter.

We made our way past the wires on our hands and knees and the three of us entered the open door of a nearby building. We sat there on the steps of the stairway, out of breath and just silently catching up with our thoughts. We sat there a long long time. When we came out again, the shots had stopped and the people had scattered. The troops were still rolling in but now they were prepared to shoot back. The crowds were leaving and my mother and I went home. It was the end of a beautiful day.

We found out later that the worst of these sniper attacks took place on the Place de Notre Dame; that's the vast plaza in front of the famous Cathedral. A large crowd had assembled there to celebrate when snipers, hiding at the top of several surrounding buildings, began to shoot randomly on the crowds; many women and little children were hurt or killed that day.

In spite of all the bloodshed of those days, the city was rocking with rejoicing and great happiness. It had been almost five long years of oppressive occupation and now life could resume again.

WHEN YOU FALL IN LOVE

After a time of adjusting to their new found freedom and jubilation, the people of Paris went back to work. My mother had sold her shop during the occupation and she now worked in an office in the Center of Paris. I still had an entire semester of school ahead of me. My schooling had greatly been interrupted by my sicknesses, my accident and also the war. My mother hired a private tutor for me. Madame Raveau was a great teacher. During the day she was math professor at the prestigious Sorbonne University. In the evening she tutored children who showed promise but who, for some reason, needed catching up. I was able to walk to her apartment twice a week after school and she drilled me in math and algebra where I was the weakest.

I was fourteen years old now and life in Paris had quickly found its own rhythm. For diversion my mother allowed me to go to some afternoon movies at the neighborhood Cine with my girlfriend Paulette or to walk her little poodle dog to the park. I could roller skate but I no longer rode my bicycle after my terrible accident. Sometimes my mother would take me out to a restaurant for dinner or to a sidewalk café for a refreshing drink.

It was September or October now and the GIs were everywhere in Paris. I could speak the little English that I was learning in school and so I was glad to help some of them find their way through the city or the subway lines. It was on a rather warm and sunny evening when my mother and I had gone shopping and were now walking the rest of the way home. We were tired and when we came to a large sidewalk café we decided to rest. It was in a very nice district of Paris and the wide sidewalks of the Avenue d'Orleans were teeming with people.

It seemed that all the little tables were occupied but we spotted a vacant one and ran for it. It was a table for four and so there were two chairs left. Two young GIs walked by and eyed the chairs. My mother motioned to them that it was alright to sit there if they wished; they smiled and sat down with us.

They were both friendly but one in particular was very young and I found myself looking at his very blue eyes. He reminded me of the dream I had earlier where the planes came down so close that and I could see the pilot's blue eyes.

My mother spoke no English at all and the conversation was far from fluent, but we did a lot of sign language and laughed a lot. They introduced themselves. One of them was Maynard, a name unfamiliar in France and hard to remember. The blue-eyed young soldier was Bill; that was easy. They asked for our names and my mother told them her name was Simone. This was not true; her name was Henriette, but I assumed that because it did not matter she felt to not give her real name. When they asked for mine she uttered "Reine" which was the name I had been called from birth, but they seemed to stumble over the pronunciation, so my mother was quick to say, "Call her Jackie." It was a name out of the blue but it was alright at the time; who knew that it would stick with me for the rest of my earthly life?

My mother was very protective of me, so after we sat and talked, mostly in charades, for a good long while, it was time to go home. She was ready to bid them good bye, but during my conversation with blue-eyed Bill I had mentioned how difficult algebra was for me and he told me that he was good at that. He offered to help me with it. There was such a genuine innocence about him; he was only nineteen.

I asked my mother if he could come and help me with my algebra and to my surprise she looked at him and agreed. His friend Maynard left and Bill walked with us to our apartment. He really helped me understand how to solve the algebra problem and quickly left to get back to his quarters on time. Before leaving he made sure to ask my mother if he could come back and visit. Surprisingly she consented.

Bill came back to see us and spent time with us mostly to help me with my algebra, geometry and also my English which was one of my important school courses…I really liked this young man and he liked me a lot too. My mother was always with us and there was absolutely no room for hanky-panky. This continued until December but after that, things took a turn.

On December 16th 1944 the strongest German offensive of the war was about to take place in the mountainous area of Belgium. The Germans had planned it in total secrecy and the strength of it took the Allies by surprise. It was the bloodiest battle the U.S forces experienced during WWII. It lasted until January 25th 1945. Ultimately the German objectives were defeated and they retreated, but I read that nineteen thousand American lost their lives; this was unsurpassed. It was known as the Battle of the Bulge.

No one we knew in Paris was aware of what was happening but right around Christmas we noticed that Bill was no longer coming to see us. We had no way to inquire about him so we could only hope that all was well. Christmas came and went and Bill never showed up. I was worried and heart broken but decided to get over it and forget him. Then one day in mid-January, a knock at the door; it was Bill. He was sorry he had not come and had not been able to contact us. Later we found out that his division had been sent to the Battle of the Bulge. Bill never talked about it but later I read on his discharged papers that he had been awarded the Purple Heart at that time.

THE GENTLEMAN FROM FLANDERS
1938

It was before the war and I was still in Southern France convalescing. My mother's busy schedule at the boutique did not leave much time for friendships or entertainment. Once in a while she enjoyed going to the "Grand Boulevards," the famed district in Paris where all the famous restaurants are located. She liked to treat herself to a nice dinner in one of these renowned places and she particularly liked the famous Tour d'Argent.

One lonely evening my mother dressed up pretty, (she was a very beautiful woman), and treated herself to this very nice restaurant. She relaxed at the little table set with the crisp white tablecloth and the nicely folded napkin. The very courteous and knowledgeable waiter explained the menu to her and she ordered her favorite dish.

As she slowly savored her food, a kitty cat came purring by her leg, begging for a little morsel of food. In France it is not unusual for the restaurant owner's pet to come and beg at the table until the owner or a waiter comes over and leads it away. Pets are treated like people in French restaurants, and the waiters will always bring a bowl of water to a dog or cat that accompanies their customer.

So this friendly kitty was busy making the rounds and found a friend in my mother who loved cats. Not far from my mother's table there was another diner by himself and the cat quickly established a "heavenly path" of delicious tidbits, going back and forth from my mother's to this gentleman's table. As the cat kept coming and going, my mother and this gentleman looked at each other and laughed.

Soon the gentleman sent the waiter to ask my mother if he could join her for dessert and coffee. She accepted and soon they shared the table and enjoyed a lively conversation. The gentleman's name was Armand. He was a bachelor from Ghent, in the Flemish region of Belgium. Belgium consists of the area of Flanders where they speak Flemish, a language similar to Dutch, and Wallones where they speak French.

My mother was about thirty-three years old at the time and Armand was about ten years older. They became good friends from the moment they met. Armand asked my mother if she would join him for dinner the following evening and she quickly accepted. He enjoyed my mother's quick wit and happy outlook on life. He was also impressed and fascinated by her keen mind and charming ways. She liked him too. He was very polite and mannerly and very intelligent as well.

Armand came to Paris once a month on business and from that day forward he made sure to call her and they went out to dinner on each of his visits. It was the beginning of a great friendship and Armand loved my mother's cheerfulness and energy. He was good for her too...she needed a true and stable friend and he was certainly all of that.

Their friendship continued for some time but in September of 1939, Hitler's Germany had declared war on Poland and in early 1940 his armies were marching into France, Belgium and Luxembourg. One of history's most destructive wars had begun. When the German armies occupied France and Belgium, they closed the borders between the two countries and no one could cross without very special permission.

Telephone communications between the two countries were silenced and there was no more mail service. From that day forward my mother never heard from her good friend Armand. She really felt bad and for a long time, she never knew whether he had been killed in one of the bombing raids over his country, or whether he was still alive and well. It was the same for Armand. This silence would last until the end of the war.

MICHEL

Michel was our lifeline during the war. He was one of my mother's customers, a widower who had raised a daughter and a son. His daughter was married and his son was about fourteen years old. Michel was probably twenty years older than my mother. He was a likeable Southern gentleman who had lived in Paris many years. As time went by, he fell madly in love with her and she liked him a lot as well. I know that she would have married him if he had asked, but because of his daughter's opposition, they just remained very close friends.

Michel was a distributor for a supply house of coffee, tea and sugar. He did business with big restaurants and cafes, and when he finished his day he usually had downed quite a few "aperitifs." Michel drank a lot, but one could never tell that he was drunk. It seemed that alcohol did not faze him, but of course it affected him a lot.

Even though coffee and sugar were high premium items during the occupation, Michel's business kept going, and a new thing called "black market" flourished. Michel was able to trade his goods for meat and cheese and all kinds of foods for his family and for my mother and me. My mother had a little closet where the aroma of coffee beans was delightful. Michel was our supplier and from time to time I would sneak out a pound of coffee or sugar and take them over to my father and Laurence who now lived in Paris too. I did not ask my mother and I do not think she ever knew about this. My heart went out to my father and his wife, I loved them dearly and I was so happy to be able to do this for them although it was not very often.

On a rainy afternoon I was in our apartment by myself as my mother was still working. A knock on the door and Michel let himself in; this was unusual. I noticed that his face was flushed. This happened often because of his drinking but this time it was more so than usual. His eyes were squinted and very shiny too. I was about twelve years old and my mother had talked to me several times about these things. She had told me, if a man comes to you and his face is flushed and his eyes are shiny…run away as fast as you can. But this was Michel…So it was different!!

I am not sure anymore how it all started but the next thing I remember is that I was laying on the bed with my panties off and he was bending over me. He was not saying anything and I wanted him to leave but he proceeded to kiss me. Then I fought him and asked him to go right now. He left.

That was all he did…nothing more. He did not physically hurt me but he wounded something deep in me, and he had violated my trust; it made me cry a lot. My mother had asked me several times if Michel had ever done anything to me and I always told her no, but now I hoped that she would not ask. I did not want to tell her because I knew that he was the provider for us, and I knew that my mother would probably be so angry that she may do something bad to him. So I never said anything to anyone ever about this—to this writing.

After that, Michel kept his distance from me. I know that he had been extremely drunk that day or he would not have done this, but I also know that if I had not resisted, it could have been a lot worse. Another time my mother sent me to deliver something to his apartment. He lived with his widowed daughter and his teen-age son. The son opened the door; he was alone and asked me in. I stepped in and he said he was doing a chemistry experiment in his room, would I come in and see it. I may have been thirteen and he was a very nice looking sixteen year old.

I went into his bedroom and he showed me his experiment. Then he closed and locked the door and had me on the bed. I had to fight tooth and nails to get free from him and run out. I was out of breath when I got home and told my mother what had happened. She faced his father but I never heard anymore about it except that my mother never sent me there again. When for some reason one of her good customers could not come to the shop, she sent me to deliver their newspaper or a small order. They were always people she knew well and for a long time.

One of my favorite places to deliver was the apartment of a couple from Martinique. In the forties, in Paris, there were very few black people and this couple was truly black. The walls of their apartment were covered with colorful tapestry and there was always an unfamiliar but pleasant spicy scent in the air. They were both very nice and it was a rare pleasure for me to deliver to them.

But now my mother was very skeptical about sending me by myself anywhere and so that was the end of that. When my mother decided something there was no arguing with her—it was final.

A PROPOSAL FROM BELGIUM

One night as we were relaxing before going to bed, my mother pulled out a long thick letter that she had received from Belgium. The borders between the two countries were still closed but the mail service was restored and with a passport and visa a person could again go through.

The letter was from her friend Armand. He could not come to Paris at the time but he had missed her terribly, and was anxious to know how she and her daughter had fared with the war. He also explained that he loved her very much and that his parents had both died. They were very strict Catholic and had been against him marrying a divorced woman. Even at his age he had respected their wishes, but now he was free to ask her to marry him.

It was December 1944. My mother's life had been very difficult. She ran her boutique while I was so sick and then because of the hardships of the war she sold it and took a job. She really liked Michel and he had been good to us, but there was no future for her with him; she knew that.

Armand was a bachelor and a businessman; he was serious. He was also what is called "Bourgeoisie" in Europe. He had two doctor's degrees in political sciences and economics. Textiles and linen are a very strong part of the Belgian economy. Armand was director of the textile union on the side of the employers. He was a man with very little time for foolishness and he had fallen in love with my mother. He desired her to be his wife. My mother was almost forty years old and ready for a well deserved rest.

Armand did not seem concerned that my mother was raising a teen age girl; that was perfectly fine with him. There were absolutely no obstacles in the way as far as he was concerned. But would my mother be willing to leave Paris... and Michel? Would she be willing to start a new life in a strange country? Was she ready for marriage after being independent for ten years?

A PIVOTAL MOMENT IN MY LIFE

A short time after she received that letter, my mother told me that she was going for a visit in Belgium. She did not want Michel to know about it because she was not sure of the outcome. What happened next would begin a series of many unexpected changes in my life. It was a gloomy day when my mother took me to a place where I was going to stay for the remainder of my school year. I had no idea that such places existed in Paris.

It was a grey stone building with a heavy gate, not far from where we lived and within walking distance of my school; it was a convent. The sisters offered room and board for young girls. There was a dormitory and a cafeteria and the girls were closely and rigidly supervised. We went to the office of the "Mother Superior" and my mother introduced us and began making all the arrangements for me to stay there until the school term was over in the spring. She also gave the "Mother" a signed letter stating that I was to leave every morning to go to school. I was to return in the afternoon as soon as school was over.

The most important part of the letter for me was that on Sundays, I was not to be forced to attend mass, but I was free to go visit my father and his wife. I had a curfew to adhere to on that day as well. I was not very happy about all this but there was nothing I could do about it and I knew that the sisters had to comply with my mother's wishes; she paid them a good amount for my keep. At the time, I attended school five days a week with Thursdays and Sundays off.

I still had the key to the apartment and if I found time I could go rest there a while. Bill was on my mind too. He had been away and if he came back he would find no one at the apartment. I had been hoping to see him again. My mother left on a Saturday and I did not have to report at the Convent until Sunday evening. I was sleeping at the apartment but with so many thoughts on my mind I did not sleep very well.

In the morning I awoke late and was still in bed when Michel walked in. He looked at me and blurted out, "Where is your mother?" He did not know, and now I had to break the news to him. I said, "She went to Belgium and I am not supposed to be here." I had told my mother that I would go to see my father but now I just did not know what I was going to do. I knew that I had to be at the Convent early that evening.

I had not thought about Michel. She had not told him about all this! I could see that he was very upset. I explained to him that she had made arrangements for me to stay at a convent until the end of the school term or until she came back; I was not sure when she would be back. I told him that I thought she was going there to get married. He left and I never saw him again. I got up and ate the quick breakfast that my mother had left for me; coffee with milk and bread and butter. I was facing the unknown and felt to just let things happen as they may.

THE CHANGES IN MY LIFE SNOWBALLED

Life at the convent was very bleak and I felt lost in the place. This was an institution which housed several girls. They were not my age and not the kind of girls that I cared to know better. The sisters were alright but of few words. The dorm was very severe with few pieces of scrubbed furnishings. Bill had given me a pack of cigarettes and that night I began to smoke. It made me dizzy and sick at first and the smell of it brought a sister to my room. I had no idea that the smoke had found its way through the entire building. Upon her demand, I put out the cigarette and then felt so bad because as she climbed the stairs back to her room, she tripped and fell and broke her elbow. It was so painful that she moaned and groaned until she was taken to the hospital by ambulance. I cried and blamed myself…things were going from bad to worse.

The following two Sundays, I was given permission to go visit my father and Laurence, but on the third one, a sister informed me that I would have to stay in. I went to Mother Superior's office and reminded her that I was supposed to visit my father on Sundays. She looked at me surprised and said that I was not permitted to do that. I explained that my mother had left a letter with permission for this, but she could not remember such a letter. I was floored!

I was not hearing from my mother and the walls seemed to be closing in on me. A feeling of dread and loneliness took hold of me; it was a very cold winter too that year. The next day, I walked to school in the snow but that afternoon I decided to go spend some time at the apartment instead of going back to the convent. I needed to see the familiar place again.

I stood in front of the door looking for the key and then I saw the note that had been stuffed in the door. It was from Bill; he was back and would like to come over to see us. He would come back late that very afternoon. What a break this was! I waited for him and he came. My heart was beating fast and I forgot all about the convent. I explained my situation to him and we went out to eat. He had to return to his base by midnight so he brought me back to the apartment; I refused to go back to the convent.

We had a nice evening together. He was barely nineteen and I was fourteen. I liked his kisses very much and he told me he loved me. It was the first time this had happened to me…and he was not too experienced either! I knew that I had put myself in danger, but I needed to be held and to be loved. I felt my heart reaching out to him. I would never be the same.

Bill left and I went to bed. I went to sleep unaware of what had been happening at the convent. The sisters were frantic. They waited for me to come home but when I did not, they immediately called my father; they had no idea that my mother had left me the key to her apartment.

My dear father told them not to worry that he would take over the responsibility of my care. That was sufficient for them; they were glad to turn the entire burden over to my father and be rid of Miss Trouble.

I was sound asleep when at about four in the morning I was awakened by a knock on the door. In my sleepiness I made my way to the door and I heard my Papa's voice, *"Open, it's me."* That was all he said. I opened the door and he came in. *"Are you alright?"* he asked with concern. *"Yes, I am just fine."* I began to cry. This was my father and I highly respected him. It was the middle of the night and he had made the trip half way across Paris just for me.

He told me to get dressed and get my things. Then he scooped up the mattress off the little day bed in the entrance way. He rolled it up and I was surprised at how easy it was for him to carry it. He was not a big man, but he showed me that he was strong. So we went to the subway station, my father, me and the mattress. There was hardly anyone on the trains at that time of the morning and we rode standing up all the way, holding the mattress, never saying a word.

My father never asked me what had happened with the sisters or why I ran away from them. He never asked me any questions and I never said anymore. I just could not help but cry and that was enough for him. I continued my school year from my father's and Laurence's place. I was happy with them. One day I told them about Bill and asked if I could see him. They said that he could come and have dinner at the house and they would be glad to meet him. Bill had given me a number where he could be reached, so I called. I had not seen him since that night at the apartment.

I told him that I was now staying with my father and his wife Laurence, and I gave him directions to meet me there. My father and Laurence could not speak English at all and Bill spoke very little French, so I was the interpreter and I was not too good at it at the time. But as the day went on with sign language and good will it was a hit. Bill felt very much at home with them. He loved my father right away and Laurence's delicious cooking really won his heart through his stomach! Bill would come and visit every evening that he was free. He kept helping me with my school work and we were a happy family.

TIME TO GO

It is only as I write this that I realize how fast things began to happen from that time on. It was in January of 1945 that I left the convent and it was in April that my mother called for me to come up and live with her and my new stepfather in Belgium. We all knew that it would come to that; my mother had custody of me and she called the shots. Also my father's apartment was not really equipped for a long term boarder; it was nice for two people but it did not have a spare bedroom. I had to sleep on the little mattress in the living room. It was time for me to leave.

The war was still not totally over and the border between France and Belgium was still closed. I did not have a passport and visa so my father gave me a signed and notarized letter to give to the agents at the border. The letter stated that my mother had custody of me and that she had moved to be with her new husband in Ghent. It stated that there was no longer any room for me to stay in France and that I belonged with her. Besides my father's letter I had a French identity card and some French francs; that was all. Because of my young age, my father was pretty certain that they would let me pass into Belgium.

The three people I loved so much took me to the train station. I said good-bye to my Dad and Laurence. Bill hugged me very tight and kissed me sweetly. I was really falling in love with him, but I had to forget about that and go to my new home. He continued his friendship and visited often with my father and Laurence; they were family.

ALONE AT THE BELGIAN BORDER

It was late Saturday evening when the Paris train pulled into the station at Lille. I was emotionally drained and physically very tired. I got off the train with my suitcase and took a room at a nearby hotel for the night.

The next morning I had a light breakfast at the hotel and went to the border with my suitcase, my father's letter and my identity card in hand. There was the French side and the Belgian side of the border.

The French gendarme understood my plight and escorted me to the Belgian officer. He handed him my card and letter and pointed out that I was only fifteen years old.

They were both very nice and kind but they looked puzzled as to what to do. The Belgian guard asked me if I had any Belgian currency. I told him no, I would need to convert some of my French money at the Bank. He quickly reminded me that this was Sunday and the banks were closed. He thought that this had solved his problem; he could not let me pass.

At that point I became very upset and told him that my mother was expecting a child and needed me. I also began to explain to him at length that my stepfather was the head of the textile unions of Belgium, and that if he loaned me money to take the trams or train to Ghent, he would quickly be refunded. I told him that my stepfather would be very grateful to him for doing this. Somehow I was able to convince this kind man to loan me money for the fare and a little to spare. He also gave me directions on how to take a series of trams to Ghent.

I thanked him profusely and gave him the name and address of my stepfather. Then I picked up my suitcase and went on my way. It was a very nice day and I really enjoyed the trip. There are no trams in Paris where we do most of our commuting by subway. I had never been on a tram before and watching the people and the scenery was very pleasant. It took several hours and several trams to get to Ghent.

Looking back at the events of that day, I know that it was the Lord that moved on the heart of that guard to give me the help I needed to arrive at my destination. However when I thought about my new life in Belgium, I felt very sad and apprehensive. I liked Paris a lot, and I would miss seeing my father and Laurence. I loved them so much...and Bill.

BEGINNING MY BELGIAN LIFE

I arrived in Ghent and found my mother's house. She knew I would soon leave Paris, but she was not sure how or when I was going to get there. The phone service between the two countries was not yet restored to the public. Mail was extremely slow and unpredictable; it was still wartime in Europe. So it was somewhat of a surprise when I rang the doorbell at my mother's house. She was several months pregnant now, and she was not feeling too good. But she seemed very glad to see me safe and sound. She was always proud of the way I handled any situation at my young age. She called me her "debrouillarde" which in French describes one who can skillfully cope with, or find their way out of any situation.

After she welcomed me and showed me my room on the third floor, my mother asked me very personal questions about my relationship with Bill. Then she said that she would be taking me to a doctor for a physical. The doctor's office was across the street from our house and it was not long until she set up the appointment. She was pleased with his good report.

I was very lonely in Belgium. I was not aware that an eleven o'clock curfew was still in force every night. The weather was nice now; spring was in the air. One night, when everyone had gone to bed I could not sleep. I was listening to American songs on the radio in my room. They were playing, "I'll never walk alone" and "I'll be seeing you." I missed Bill a lot; we had such a good rapport and I was always so happy in his company. We were both so very young, yet we could talk of so many interesting things. I missed his kiss too and his comforting arms around me. And I missed the times we had together with my father and Laurence. Those memories were alive in my mind.

I looked out the window and saw that it was very light that night; there was a beautiful full moon and many stars in the sky. I tiptoed downstairs so I would not wake anyone. I found the key and went out the door. The streets were totally emptied, (I did not know about the curfew). About a block away was a canal with benches along the way where one could sit and relax. It was such a beautiful night and I felt such longing within that I needed to identify with something that was familiar. The moon and stars and the smells of the night did just that. I had begun to smoke with Bill and I sat on a bench and lit a cigarette.

Little did I realize that the bench where I sat was directly across from the police station. The lights were on and I saw policemen walking out. Two of them approached me and said something in Flemish. I answered them in French so one of them spoke French and asked what I was doing on the bench. I explained that I lived close by and just needed some fresh air. He explained the curfew to me and escorted me back to the door of my house.

I anxiously tried the key that I had grabbed on my way out, and lo and behold, it was the wrong key. The policeman suggested ringing the bell but I was terrified of waking up my stepfather and having to explain my situation as I stood at the door with a policeman bringing me home; I refused to ring the bell. The policeman seemed to understand my dilemma and took me back to the police station where I spent the night.

The next morning I was free to go home but I still had to ring the doorbell and explain the whole story to my mother. At least Armand had left for his office and I did not have to face him. I am not sure whether my mother told him or not; I assumed that she did. A couple of weeks later, I was in for a surprise. Armand had received a letter from the police with a fine for violating the curfew. It all came out and I apologized for my costly escapade. My days in Ghent were very sad; I was homesick. I did not feel that I belonged in that country, in that house or that I was part of that family.

On May 8, 1945 Victory Day for all Europe was announced with great jubilee in the streets and with the ringing of all church bells everywhere. It was VE day, the end of the war in Europe. That night there were celebrations in the streets of Ghent and I joined in some of the marching around the blocks with young people. But my heart remained sad.

Shortly after that, I received a letter from Bill. He was no longer needed in Europe but the war in the Pacific theater was still raging. He was going to be sent out to that area very soon. It was as if a sheet of ice just wrapped around me and I felt fear. I was so afraid that I would never see him again.

Bill had been visiting my father and Laurence regularly; they had become good friends. I wrote my father and shared my heart with him. I asked if I could come and stay with them for a while so that I could see Bill before he shipped out.

My father wrote a letter to my mother inviting me to come to Paris for the summer. There was a lot of animosity between my mother and father because of many things that had taken place between them concerning me, but in spite of that my mother consented. I am sure she had easily detected my melancholy and may have been concerned for my health. The big problem now was that the border between France and Belgium was still closed. This meant that no passport could be issued unless it was for an approved good reason; there would be no way of getting back to France. This approval, if it was given at all, would take weeks to be granted. We were in the part of Belgium that is Flemish and there is a real undercurrent against French speaking people in that part of the country; at least that was the way at the time.

ATTEMPTING TO CROSS THE BORDER AGAIN AND AGAIN

What took place next is a story for the books as they say. It may even appear that I made it up, but it really happened. My mother was forty-years old and about six months pregnant; it showed. She tired easily, but nevertheless she decided that she would help me get back to Paris. She knew I was so unhappy there. We packed lightly and she took the letter of invitation that my father had sent me. She was sure that she could explain the situation to the guard at the border. She was certain that we would have no problem. My mother was always great when facing a challenge.

Mail coming from France was still randomly censored, so before leaving Ghent, a friend of my mother's handed her a letter and asked her to mail it for her in France. My mother thought nothing of doing her that favor and put the letter in her purse. We took the train to the border. There are several places where one can cross the border and this was at a different place than where I had entered.

At the border, my mother requested to talk to the person in command, so we were escorted inside to the office where a guard sat behind his desk. We were not invited to sit down so my mother began telling my story and showing him my father's letter. The only problem was that she accidentally handed him the wrong letter. It was the one that this "friend" had given her to mail in France and not my father's letter.

We never found out what was in that letter. But as it was the chief became very angry with us and began questioning our true intentions. It was all my mother could do to talk her way out of this situation. We walked out and headed back home. We did not make it over the border that day but we did not give up. There would be another day.

AN INCREDIBLE DAY

It may have been a week or two later, I cannot remember for certain, but my mother had a plan. She was a master at solving difficult situations and she was determined to see this to the finish.

She informed herself about the possibilities of crossing the border without a passport and she found out that a certain area of the border was deserted, out in the country side. Guards patrolled the road back and forth with their dogs but at certain times they changed shifts. There was an all night diner on the border, and they knew the times that the guards changed shifts. Someone could quickly run across the fields to France between the time that one guard left and the other arrived on duty. It had been done many times. This was the information that my mother gathered. She did not give anyone any details at the time, but late one night, we took the train to the border again.

It was before dawn when we arrived and found the diner. This time, we had left home without suitcases; we wore two layers of clothing just to have a clean change. We sat at the counter and we ordered a hot drink. My mother gave the waitress a generous tip and in turn she casually told us that the night guard was about to leave his post. We would have several minutes before the next guard and his dog came on duty.

We quickly went out the door and found our way through the field. It was still dark and we walked very fast. We could see the light of the

French border town ahead of us; it was quite a distance. We never looked back and before we knew it we were walking on the cobblestones of the little French town across the border. There were no guards or custom booth at that point of the French border; we had made it. We found an open café and sat down for breakfast.

After eating and resting a while we felt refreshed and hailed a taxi to the railroad station. There would be a train for Paris later that day; we waited. The train came. It was several hours to Paris. My mother still had the key to her apartment and we went there and rested. Then I called my father and told him of our experience. He was so happy that I was back and we arranged for my coming to his house. At the same time my mother made her arrangements for a train to return to Belgium. I stayed with my mother.

The next day we arranged for my father and Laurence to meet us at the railroad station where my mother was to board the train back home. She would tell another story to get back in Belgium, but this time it would be easy. I was very happy to be back near my father.

We arrived at the Gare du Nord and found that Bill had come along with my father and Laurence. We were early so we all went into the restaurant for coffee. It was there that things took a turn and my mother and father had a very big argument. It was about the savings bankbook that my mother was holding for me. The account was in my name and could only be cashed by me after the age of twenty-one. When my father sold his house in Aulnay, he had deposited a portion of the money as an inheritance for me in that account. He and my godfather Francois had also made regular deposits along the years.

It was on that day at the railroad station that my father asked my mother to turn the book over to him; she refused. She must have anticipated this because she had the book in her purse. Finally after getting quite nasty, she handed the book over to him. My father who was always a quiet; reserved man could no longer contain himself. He took the book and threw it back at her saying, "She will never need this!" These words turned out to be prophetic. (Actually my mother mailed me the book years later and I was able to cash it and pay some bills.)

When I went to kiss my mother goodbye, she turned away and slapped my face. She had never done this before but she was so angry with me for causing this entire situation. Now I understand her deep concern for me, but then I was a stubborn teenager and also in retrospect I know that I was following my destiny in Christ. I know now that this was the way that my heavenly Father had chosen for me from the foundation of the world.

A SIGNIFICANT TURN IN MY LIFE

It was so nice to be with my father and Laurence again. Bill came to visit frequently. Laurence was a great cook and Bill enjoyed helping her in the kitchen; he loved to cook too and he was learning how to make many good dishes. Bill was now in charge of the PX for the troops in Paris so he had access to a lot of good things. He was very generous with us and shared the bounties that he could buy very inexpensively on base.

It must have been a Sunday in June or early July when Bill came over with a very troubled look on his face. Although by now he was able to express himself a little in French, I needed to interpret this serious piece of news. Bill was explaining that because the war in Europe was over, many were now being called to the war in the Pacific theater. Bill's training and expertise were in communications, his unit was needed to give relief in that area. He was now awaiting his orders to be transferred to the Pacific. He had no idea how long this would take, but he knew that it would not be very long.

We looked at each others with stunned faces; somehow we had not expected this so soon. Bill continued explaining with tears welling up in his eyes—it was not a matter of if, it was a matter of when he would leave and he would not be sent back to Europe. When the time came for him to be discharged he would be sent home to South Bend Indiana; he would have no way of sending for me. In those days travel from one continent to the other was very expensive and there would be a long wait to obtain a visa that might not be granted. There were too many obstacles and only one solution.

Bill had thought about this and decided that there was only one sure way that we would be re-united; he wanted to marry me as soon as possible. He explained that although we were both too young by normal standards, yet the situation called for unusual means. Marriage was the only way to assure my possibility of joining him later in the States. This way he could send for me as his wife. It made sense. Bill was asking my father for my hand in marriage. They looked at me and I stared at them.

I felt as if I was caught in a whirlwind. I really wanted to marry Bill but I had not thought of it happening this soon. Looking back on all this, although I did not comprehend any of it at the time, I am convinced that this was all God's plan for my life. In the meantime, my father said that he would have to think about it and that we would talk about it again; and we did.

In France, the minimum age for marriage with parental permission is fifteen years and three months for a girl. It was July and I was fifteen and five months. My father contacted my mother and she was absolutely against it. Even if my father approved it, she would never come to the wedding. So it was left solely in my father's hands and above all, although I was not personally aware of this, it was left in my heavenly Father's Hand.

AN ENORMOUS DECISION

When Bill came to visit on his following time off, my father was ready to let us all know his final decision. My father was a man of great understanding, but most of all he was a man who loved God and read his Bible. He did not like church and never went, but he was an avid reader of the Book of Revelation and would often discuss its meaning with Laurence. I am sure he had prayed and sought God for this. My father agreed that Bill and I should not lose track of each other. Because Bill was about to be shipped out to a very distant place and would not have the means to come back to Paris, he felt that by my being his wife, he could legally send for me. In other words, my father was putting his seal of approval for his fifteen year old daughter to marry this young man who had just turned twenty. Bill and I were elated.

There was not much time to plan a wedding so it would be very simple. At any rate there would not be many people attending; it was to be a wedding mainly for the legality of it all. Bill wrote his mother and gave her our ring sizes; she purchased and sent us two plain gold wedding bands. Because Bill was not twenty-one, he had to get permission from his commanding officer; he did this.

At the time in Paris, all Christian churches were Roman Catholic with the exception of very few, so Bill and I went to talk to a priest in a Catholic Church; Bill was Methodist and came from a staunch Methodist family. The priest told us that because Bill was not Catholic, we would have to be married in the "sacristy" rather than in front of the main altar. That was not too objectionable but when the priest told him that in order to marry in the Church he would have to sign a paper promising to raise his children Catholic, he flatly refused. That was the end of that.

After that my father, who was well acquainted with Paris, went on a hunt for what may have been the only Lutheran Church in Paris. He found this nice little church in the center of the city; it was ideal. Quickly, Laurence and I went shopping for a nice outfit and I found a very pretty powder pink suit with a beautiful silky blouse; I liked it a lot.

We went for the marriage license and they published the "bans" at City Hall. That was the custom for all who married. A list of the names of those who had applied for a marriage license was published in the newspapers and posted on the bulletin board of City Hall for ten days. During that time, anyone who had an objection could come forth and be heard.

On August 2nd of 1945 Bill and I were married in that little Lutheran Church in Paris in front of God and my family. I still felt as if I was caught in a whirlwind without control of the situation. After a very nice dinner, Bill had to report to base. He promised me a honeymoon in Hawaii later but that never happened! He was still waiting for his orders to be shipped out. But now I was his wife and I was on the list of war brides to be shipped to the U.S. later.

Bill and I began our married life in a small efficiency apartment on "Rue d'Italie" in Paris. He spent most of his time on duty and I went to market for fresh meat and vegetables and learned to cook. I quickly fell into the role of housewife and really liked it. On the weekends that Bill was off, we often went out with two other couples like us. One of them was Maynard, the friend who had been with Bill when we first met at the café. Maynard was probably in his early thirties; he was from Rhode Island. He had married a very nice French girl with the same reasoning that Bill and I did; he was waiting to be shipped out to the Pacific theater. The six of us would often go out and enjoy some of the Paris night life; we drank and danced and as they say, "we had a ball!"

PIERROT

It was shortly after the Germans left Paris that my adopted brother Pierrot knocked on my father's door. He had spent three years in German forced labor camp and had escaped through perilous ways. He had found his way to Italy and then up to France with the help of several families along the way. When my father opened the door, he did not recognize the bearded, smelly, ragged individual that stood there; he was a sick man. My father and Laurence took him in, bathed him and put him to bed. There was a nurse in the building and they called on her to come and see him.

It took a long time but with their great love and care Pierrot recovered and was back on his feet. When he was taken to the labor camp he was a healthy young man with a wife who was about four months pregnant. Now his little daughter who looked just like him was three years old. However Pierrot had totally changed; he was not the same person. He rejected his wife with all sorts of false accusations and denied that little Laurencette was his daughter, even though she looked just like him. It was very sad.

Then Pierrot proceeded to look for his biological family. He found out that his mother was from a town in Eastern France called Besancon and he was able to find her. He soon found out that she was from a rich family and wanted absolutely nothing to do with him. He then announced to Yvette that he was divorcing her and leaving for Algeria. This is exactly what he did. My father was devastated.

In the early fifties, my father and his wife moved out of Paris and went to live near Laurence's home town of Soulac-sur Mer on the Atlantic Coast. Shortly after that, my father took a trip to Algeria to try to find his son. He found him but when Pierrot answered the door he held a gun and told his father that he must leave him alone. He wanted nothing to do with his previous life.

That was the result of his stay in the German labor camp. I have never heard from Yvette or Laurencette since I left France and my father never mentioned them. I asked my father for Pierrot's address and wrote to him, but I received the same response. He loved me but desired to be left alone. If he is still alive at this writing he is eighty-five years old.

Laurence was very happy in Soulac but soon I began receiving news from her explaining that she was in a lot of pain. Not long after that, she passed away. My father explained that she had suffered from ovarian cancer. Laurence was buried with her family in Soulac and my father returned to Paris.

One day my father decided to call on one of his colleagues of many years. When the wife Georgette answered the call, she told him that her husband had died. I was not told the details of how Georgette and my father got together but he soon told me that he was getting married again. They moved in an apartment on Rue Cler, a street famous for its market, bakeries and specialty shops of all kinds. Every day, my father went to the market to buy fresh fruit and vegetables, and chat and kibitz with the vendors. He was now about sixty-eight years old and still a strong man. He had chosen to live his old age in peace. He had done his best.

Thine is the great Light
guiding me into safe harbors...
(Diana Summers)

ACT TWO

From Paris to Florida by way of Indiana

1946-1956

WORLD WAR II IS OVER!

The Army newspaper, "Stars and Stripes," said it in letters as big as the front page, **"THE WAR IS OVER!"** Bill and I had been married only a week when it happened. The **WAR WAS OVER!** On August 9th 1945 the Americans had dropped the atom bomb on Hiroshima, and that was the end of the story. As a result, Bill did not have to leave France to go to the Pacific. I was elated, but by the same token, my life as a full time wife began a lot sooner than I expected. This was August of 1945 and Bill continued at his post running the PX in Paris; life was good.

In January of 1946, I knew that I was pregnant; our first child would be born in September. We were both happy about that but there was a serious problem and I was the only one who knew about it. Bill had episodes of moods that were frightening to me. At one point, I packed my suitcase to go stay with my grandmother. I thought I would confide in her, but Bill caught up with me at the subway station and talked me into coming back. I loved him dearly and was hoping that all would somehow work out.

Once, Bill did something that was very difficult for me to forgive, but I was pregnant and I did not want to disappoint my father and Laurence. There was no way that I would tell my mother; we did not communicate. I had a heavy heart but I was so young and full of hope anyway.

One night I had a dream that stayed with me for many days. In the dream *I was aboard a large ship and it was the middle of the night. I was up on deck and looked in the distance. I could see lines of bright lights and buildings taller than I had ever seen before; I felt so alone and afraid. But then I heard a strong but loving voice say to me "Don't be afraid, you are in New York City now." This voice seemed to calm my fears.*

At the end of February 1946 Bill received his orders; he would be shipping home the first of March. Then I received my papers and was told to get my police records (in case I had a criminal record!), health certificate from a doctor and a passport ready. I would be leaving for

New York at the end of March.

This was going to be extremely difficult for me; I was about to leave everyone and everything I knew. I really loved Paris too, but most of all I would be leaving my very dear parents and Memere. We all went to a photographer to have some nice pictures made. Then Bill and I decided to take a quick trip up to Belgium to say goodbye to my mother and my baby brother Jean-Pierre who was now four months old.

I do not remember the exact date that I left Paris for Cherbourg, but it was a cold, rainy day in March. Bill was already back in the U.S. He was going to meet me on my arrival in South Bend, Indiana. In Cherbourg, the American Army had set up barracks where the war brides were processed for their voyage to the U.S. Each camp was named after a brand of cigarettes. I was in Camp Philip Morris. It was there that we received all our shots and we were given our final physical examinations.

LONG JOURNEY TO A STRANGE LAND

We were war brides now and we had to stay in barracks in the camp. We were treated like GIs and were told that we were to obey the rules just as our husbands did. Then we boarded a ship, the SS. Zebulon B.Vance. It was a converted "Liberty ship" that had been used as an army hospital ship during the war. Now it was purposely equipped to bring the first load of French and English war brides to the U.S.

I was four months pregnant by that time. The fifteen days and fifteen nights I spent on a very stormy ocean in March was not the most enjoyable ride I have ever taken. I was blessed because, although I came close to it a few times, I did not really get seasick. Some war brides spent the entire voyage in the hospital part of the ship.

Red Cross nurses tended to our care and kept us entertained. They taught us the song, *"My Bonnie lies over the ocean..."* The voyage took a long fifteen days because there were still German mines on the shortest route, so our ship had to go around what they called the great "Northern Circle;" it seemed endless.

Finally on April 4th, 1946, the ship came into the waters a few miles out of the New York Harbor. It was the middle of the night and I had been asleep in my bunk when I heard everybody getting up to go up on deck. When I got on top deck the night was very bright; every star and the moon were out to welcome the little ship. A crisp chilly wind was softly blowing and the roar of the engines had been silenced; the ship was standing still. I was wearing my nice, soft beaver fur jacket and I thrust both my hands in the pockets to keep warm. My heart was racing; it was a mixture of fear and excitement.

Then I looked right in front of the ship, in the distance, and there they were, just as in my dream: the lights of the skyscrapers of New York City. Suddenly I could hear the voice again, *"You are in New York City now..."* and again fear left me; I was comforted; I knew that this was where I was supposed to be. This was my new country now.

NEW YORK CITY

In the morning the U.S. customs agents boarded our ship and it was not long until the tug boats escorted us into the harbor. Much to my surprise, there were hundreds if not thousands of people on the pier. They were all smiling and waving to welcome us. I was amazed at the colorful clothing they wore; the day was beautiful...warm and sunny. When we left France it was stormy and cold. I was still dressed for the cold and had not expected this warm sunny weather in New York. I was wearing my favorite royal blue dress and my fluffy beaver jacket. I had a chic turban hat on my head. This was the outfit that I had picked for my arrival; all my other clothes were packed in my trunk and would be transferred directly to the train for South Bend.

We were told that the mayor of New York City, Mayor LaGuardia, was boarding the ship to give a welcome speech. We were the first boat of war brides coming to the United States after the war. We were made to feel like important people!!

Everything was moving so fast now. I was tired and felt lost and so inadequate. My English had been good for Bill and our friends, but now it seemed that everyone spoke so fast that it was hard to understand. Bill had already been discharged from the service. He was waiting for me in South Bend. On that day, I really missed him.

SOUTH BEND INDIANA

The Red Cross took us off the ship and to the bus that drove us to Grand Central Station. We had cards with our names and destination on our lapels and we just followed the leaders. Not everyone was going in the same direction, but in Grand Central Station I was led to board the train to Chicago and South Bend, Indiana. I was given a small amount of money for my meals aboard the train, but the currency was all strange to me and I had no idea of the value of the coins.

It was a very rough ride on the train because for fifteen days and fifteen nights my body had gotten used to the up and down rolls of the waves. Now the train was rocking me from side to side. I really felt sea sick now. I was assigned a very nice sleeping berth, and even though it was still afternoon, I went to bed. Later, I felt better and made my way to the dining car for a bite to eat. Looking back on it later, I think I tipped the kind waiter with one of my nickels! But who knew!

The train was due to arrive in South Bend at noon the next day. I settled in my berth for the night. For some unknown reason, the large window by my bed had slightly rolled down. In the middle of the night I was awakened when the train made an abrupt stop. The signs said that we were in Buffalo NY.

All of a sudden a billow of heavy dark smoke came through the window and covered my bed. I blew my nose; it was all black! So I rang for the attendant and I was directed to a shower and another berth. That incident sure broke the monotony!! The next morning the train pulled into Chicago and the next stop would finally be my destination.

Around eleven the conductor told me that we would be arriving in less than an hour. It was just about noon on a bright and sunny April 5, 1946 that the train from New York City pulled into the station at South Bend, Indiana. I had my royal blue dress with the sequin collar on, and my turban hat on my head! I must have looked quite strange to all the people who were waiting on the quay. The South Bend Tribune was there to take pictures too. As I came down the steps of the train I looked and saw Bill running toward me; we were so happy to be together again.

The reason the newspaper people were there to take my picture was not because I was rich or famous but simply because I was the first war bride from Paris that they ever saw. They must have been amused as I stood in my pretty royal blue dress with sequins, my chic turban hat, and my beaver fur jacket on my arm. It had been cold winter when I left France and now it was a warm sunny spring day. Everyone on the quay was in short sleeves; I felt out of place but most of all I was uneasy.

After a good hug and kiss, Bill picked up my suitcase and we went to claim the rest of the baggage. Then he brought me to our new car; it was a used car but it was a very nice light blue Oldsmobile. Wartime had halted the production of new cars and people had to get on a list to get one when ready. Bill put his name on several lists and two years later we were able to buy a brand new 1948 Jeep Station Wagon.

Bill brought me to his mother's house. She lived with his two sisters and a brother about my age. It was the beginning of many trials and difficulties for me. I will skip all the details on my life there. I know I was terribly homesick. There were times when I locked myself in my room so no one would see me crying my heart out. But I was not going to give in to despair and I made up my mind to just move on.

Shortly after I arrived in April, Bill's older sister Norma wisely decided that I should be under a doctor's care for my pregnancy, so she took me to their family physician. Dr. Arisman was a nice old fashioned practitioner; I was in good hands. I was told to expect my baby September 8th; Anita was born on September 4th 1946.

Bill was a good worker. He had a steady job at Sears repairing radios. Later when televisions came out, Sears sent him to school in Chicago and he learned to fix them too. He was extremely smart. Later he was hired as an engineer for Bendix Aviation where he was part of a team that designed and tested missile guidance systems for the space program.

It was about July when we moved from Bill's mother's house and rented a small house in the suburbs of South Bend. Bill never showed his temper in front of anyone, but after we moved on our own, things began to get more difficult. Even though Bill really loved me, his episodes of violent temper were happening more often and were becoming more of a danger to me. They happened when least expected and I was afraid of him. After a violent incident, he would cry and was very sorry. He would bring me long stemmed roses and promise that it would never happen again. I tried to believe him, but things did not change.

Anita was born in September. She was the most beautiful baby girl anyone ever saw. Not only was she beautiful, she was an angel. The family came to the hospital to see her. They loved her and were very good to her.

As Anita grew, she was very obedient and always wanted to please. She was just a few months old when we bought a piece a land in the country and Bill set up one of those prefab building that were so popular after the war. It was just large enough for our little family. It was a rude building with no running water or electricity, but it was livable while we waited to build a nice house on the property.

The first winter was hard. We had to carry our water in buckets from the neighbor's house and I had to wash diapers by hand. We finally got electricity and a pump, but on the many days and nights below zero the pump would freeze. Bill worked hard at trying to keep us comfortable but it was not easy. We had an oil drum outside and a good oil furnace inside. It would keep us warm as long as oil was delivered, or as long as the wind did not come down the flue and blow the flame out of the furnace. All these discomforts meant nothing to me. It was the violence that flared up so often that distressed me.

The following February I became pregnant again. The doctor predicted that the baby would be born on November 15th. Our little son was born on November 17th of 1947. Jon Alan was the tallest baby that this doctor ever delivered—23 inches long and he weighed seven pounds thirteen ounces; for me that was a large baby. Now our family was complete. These two children were going to have a hard start in life, but they proved to be overcomers with bright minds and good attitudes.

As Bill became more and more violent with me, I was caught in a downward spiral. I was extremely thin and anemic and I truly did not know where to turn. In those days there was no such thing as help for abused wives; things like that were kept in the closet. Bill was so nice to everybody that no one suspected such a thing, and I would never tell; I was too afraid of the repercussions.

NIGHT FELL AND DAY LIGHT DID NOT RETURN

It was not long after I arrived in this country that I entered the darkest time of my life. It was as if a black curtain fell over me and I had no way out; I could not find myself anymore. Bill had inexplicable moods of violence and I was frightened. I knew that my marriage was in big trouble. I had come from a divorced family and my greatest desire was to give my children what I had not had myself. My childhood had been very lonely, not only because I had been so sick and so long in hospitals, but also because my heart so yearned to have a home with a father and a mother as most of the children I knew. Now my dreams were shattered.

I was blessed because both my children were perfect and healthy. Anita was a little jewel, and Jon was a real boy and a great joy in my life. When Bill and I had been married five or six years, things began to get so violent that I knew something must be done. It had all been a well guarded secret, and even our close friends and his family (mother, two sisters and a brother) did not seem to be aware of it. All my family was in Europe and I certainly did not mention anything to them in my letters.

After my son was born I had lost so much weight that I became very anemic; I knew that now my health was in jeopardy. The love I had once felt for Bill was now replaced by fear and dread. He was still very nice and loving in his old ways, but I dreaded the times when he lost his temper and became extremely violent with me over such little things as “I did not cook supper to his liking” or for no reason at all. The episodes of violence were coming closer and closer together and I knew that this could not last.

Our children were a blessing to me and to Bill too. He loved them dearly and was not violent with them as he was with me, although he was a tough disciplinarian and I did not approve of that. When I mentioned having to leave him, he declared that if I left and took the children he would find us and it would be hell to pay…whatever that meant, I was terrified at the thought.

ANITA AND JON ALAN

Bill always went to work and had been good to provide for us, but the time came when the State of Indiana allowed slots machines in private clubs. Bill belonged to the DAV and they purchased a few of those "one arm bandits." He loved them and would stop there on pay day to have a few drinks and play the slot machines. As a result our bills were no longer paid on time. We were still living in the prefab garage that was turned into a little dwelling for us. We still hoped to be able to someday build a house in front but with Bill's new found love for slot machines, the hope for this was quickly fading.

Gambling was a new thing with Bill and he gambled a lot of the money we needed. It was when our electricity was cut off because we could not pay the bill that I made the decision to look for a job. I first applied at the Studebaker factory to see if by chance they could use a French interpreter or translator; they already had one and he was not going to leave for a long time.

Then, an acquaintance of Bill offered me a job at the busy lunch counter of a drugstore in town. I quickly became a "soda jerk" and learned to make milk shakes, malted milks, sodas, sundaes and banana splits too. I had never even heard of these things but I was willing to learn. I also learned to flip hamburgers on the grill and make tuna fish salad sandwiches. It paid little but I enjoyed working with the public, and it was my breakthrough in this new world. I now look back and know that God was in it all although at the time I felt so alone.

I found a lady to take care of my children. Her name was Betty and she kept children while their parents worked. So the arrangement seemed suitable. I am not sure how long I worked at the drugstore when another job opened up. It was at the newly built airport building; a restaurant named Dobbs House was looking to hire waitresses. I applied and there I met a woman who was actually a neighbor and was very willing to teach me the ropes. She taught me how to carry those large silver trays stacked with heavy restaurant platters.

They had to be stacked in such a way so that they were well balanced and the dishes did not slide off. She was left handed so she taught me to carry left handedly!! In a few months I became very good at this job and I did pretty well with tips too. The airport was not far from my house and my new found friend Ferrell said I could always ride with her. I could drive but we only had the one car and Bill needed it to go to work. Through life, God always has someone there to help with the load. Ferrell was my angel at the time.

MY FIRST MOVE TO FREEDOM

Things were not getting better at home. The violence continued to get worse. Bill had frequent fits of uncontrollable anger and it was all directed at me; no one else seemed to trigger his anger but me. After each bout, Bill would be very remorseful and cry. Each time he bought me long-stemmed red roses and asked my forgiveness proclaiming his love. That was the pattern and the hope that kept me there for seven years. Betty, the lady who kept our children was moving to a place farther out in the country. I felt I could make my move and Bill would not find the children. I visited an attorney and he drew up divorce papers. At this juncture I moved to my friend Ferrell's house. She and her husband had a nicely furnished basement and they offered to let me stay there a while.

It was not long until Bill found me and to my surprise he was not violent or even angry. He was crying and repentant and bought me the traditional long stemmed red roses as he often did after a beating. He was always so sorry that he had hurt me and told me how much he really loved me; I knew that he was sincere at the time, but… He promised as he had so many times that he would never hurt me again. I wanted to believe him this one more time. I wanted it for myself and for my children and I felt sorry for him. So we kissed and made up again. I brought the children home and cancelled the divorce action.

I have no idea how long it was before the fits of anger returned worse than ever; but this time I could no longer cope. I was rising up in self defense and becoming violent myself; I was ready to kill him. My own frustration and anger against him were evolving in a way that scared me more than his ever did. I had to leave.

However, I waited a year longer to make my move. My children had been getting a lot of sore throats and the doctor wanted to take their tonsils out as soon as the youngest one was five. He had suggested that both have that surgery at the same time and we agreed. I knew that it had to be done while I could still benefit from Bill's work insurance. So when Jon turned five and Anita was six, I took them for the surgery and soon their general health improved a great deal.

After that I went back to work while the children stayed securely with their grandmother. I knew that I did not have to worry about them with her. She lived in town and within walking distance of a school. We enrolled them and they stayed at her house around the clock. Bill had access to them and would not fail to support them. This brought peace to my heart. This time my mind was made up no matter what. I was now twenty-two years old and had a job serving breakfast in the dining room of the nicest hotel in town. I rented a room at a boarding house for ladies only. I could use the kitchen if needed, but because I worked at a nice hotel dining room I was getting two good meals a day there. I was not thinking about the future but for the time being this would work. Bill could not come to see me where I lived as men were not allowed on the premises. As a matter of fact he must have sensed my determination and this time he did not try.

I have many more memories of this time of my life, but because it personally involves others beside me, I choose to skip the details of those days. I am certain of one thing– the same God who had spoken to me about my coming to this country– the same God who kept me from harm during the war in France– the same God who saved my leg from amputation– yes somehow I knew that this same God was with me. I prayed and cried myself to sleep many nights, but somehow I could feel His presence and I knew that He was taking care of all things—especially my children.

FLORIDA BOUND

In 1948, on my son's first birthday, I became an American citizen. It was on that occasion that I met a couple of French women who were also war brides. Both of them were also named Jackie. One of them, with her husband Stanley, became good friends of Bill and me. Jackie, my children and I spent a lot of time on weekends together while our husband often went fishing in Michigan. Later when I was divorced, I rented a little apartment in town. Jackie was having problems and stayed with me for a while. The apartment was within walking distance from down town where I worked and where she worked also. I had a good job at a very nice new pizza restaurant called "The Volcano." She worked in an office.

After a while Jackie divorced and remarried. She and her new husband decided to move to Florida. At that time, my health was deteriorating. I was having frequent bouts of strept throats and was often very sick, having to take penicillin. My old faithful family doctor said it was serious because it was a sign that my immune system was down. He advised me to leave South Bend and go some place like Arizona if at all possible. I was divorced now and my children were staying with their grandmother; this was the best arrangement it seemed, except that it turned sour when I had to make the very painful decision of moving. I was hoping that my mother in law would keep the children until I was settled somewhere, but that proved to be much more difficult than I had anticipated.

I felt desperate with no one to turn to. Laurence had passed away and my father had moved back to Paris. He had married Georgette who was also widowed from his long time colleague and friend. My mother was happy with her little son (my half brother) Jean-Pierre and her husband Armand in Belgium.

I had not confided in any of them because I knew that it would hurt them and frustrate them as they could do nothing to help me. There was no such thing as help for battered women that I knew of at the time, and I had no idea that I could turn to the government for some kind of help; that did not even enter my mind. I only knew I was on my own.

My doctor had mentioned perhaps moving to Arizona but that was not to be. Then Jackie and her husband made plans to move to Florida and they offered to take me along. Looking back I know that it was all God's plan in my life, but I did not know it at the time. Jackie had a brother who had just arrived from France. Her mother lived near where my father lived in Paris and so when Jackie introduced her brother Jacques to me we became friends. He could speak very little English and I was able to help him with that. He was a nice, neat looking young man and we were the same age.

We arrived in Hollywood Florida and rented a duplex. I immediately looked for work and found a job as a waitress. It was not easy to break through in Florida with just the experience that I had. During that time I took a train back to South Bend to visit the children. I missed them terribly. I was not sure I would be able to stay in Florida so far away from them. I knew I could easily get my job back where I had worked before but when I got to South Bend it was the middle of winter and very cold. I fell sick again. I took a room in a hotel until I was well enough to find my way back to Florida. The children were doing fine considering.

MOVING ALONG IN FLORIDA

When I returned to Florida I knew I must get a better job and move out on my own. I found out about a French restaurant in Dania. I went to see if I could get work there but they hired only waiters. As I was leaving one of the French waiters came out to tell me that his wife Bessie worked at a nice restaurant nearby. It was a fancy steak house called the "Cock and Bull." He suggested that I go see Bessie because they needed help.

So I went and met Bessie. She was a tall strong woman from Alabama. She was very pleasant and as the head waitress, she saw to it that I was hired on the spot. I found a little studio apartment a block away, so I was within walking distance of my job. Bessie showed me the ropes. She was very good for me because she could do the heavy work of lifting the trays and I was good for her because I could speedily take the customers' orders and take care of the checks. I was also very well liked by the customers because of my French accent and I was pleasant to look at. Bessie and I were a team!

Life continued for me at the Cock and Bull during the entire winter season. In the Summer I resorted to a job at the counter of a nearby drug store. The place was busy with teenagers coming in to eat burgers and play the juke box. It met my need.

After a couple of years, the Cock and Bull closed its doors and Bessie and I were without a job. They were looking for good dining room waitresses at the Chateau Motel on Miami Beach. Bessie and I went to apply and got the job right away. The executive Chef and manager was a Frenchman called Marcel. He was an excellent cook but very high strung.

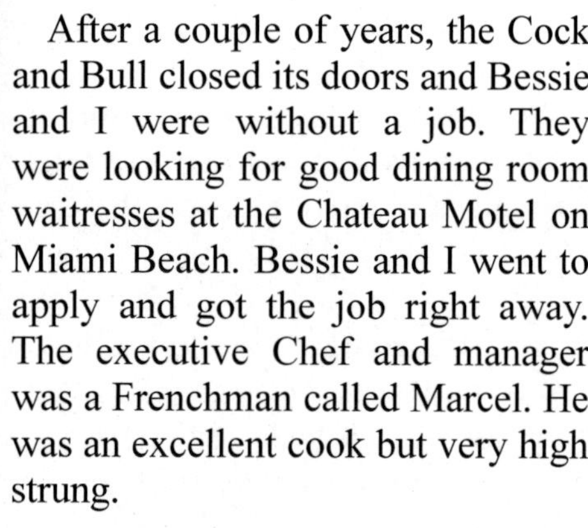

BESSIE AND ME
A team

Bessie and I worked only a few weeks when the paychecks that Marcel handed out began to bounce. Then one afternoon the police came to arrest him. He had been dealing drugs and now he was in trouble. This was the end of Marcel for us. The owners of the Chateau quickly hired another Chef. This man was a French speaking Lebanese by the name of Maurice. He came from New York with his right hand man who took care of the cash register, as well as checking everything that went out of the kitchen. This man's name was Michael.

The owners of the Chateau were quick to tell Chef Maurice that whatever he did, he must keep Bessie and me on his staff. This was part of the deal!! So Maurice hired his new crew but kept us and a couple of others as well. The kitchen was perking again but this time it was well organized. Maurice was a superb chef. He knew how to twirl the ends of his little mustache and execute the French dishes that the customers raved about.

Michael was a very important man in the kitchen. He checked every dish and platter that left the kitchen and also made sure that everything was on the tab. He also rejected anything that did not look as good as it should; this man knew his job well. He was very serious and kept his desk and the area around his cash register in meticulous order. He was fast, efficient, and pleasant, but a man of few words.

For some reason I felt comfortable around that man. Perhaps it was just that I liked his impeccable work; it made my job easier. But there was more; somehow I was attracted to his looks, his cleanliness, his manners. He was not as other men around young women; he was respectful and kind. Perhaps without my being aware of it, he reminded me of my father.

It was September of 1956 and the busy winter season had just begun; we stayed busy and worked hard every day. I worked hard, seven days a week and I kept up that schedule for several months. I had my little apartment in Dania and a little Dodge Rambler convertible that I had bought from my landlord. It ran like a charm. I picked up Bessie every morning and we worked lunch and dinner. At night I would fall asleep watching the late night show with Jack Paar. That was pretty much my life.

He who dwells in the secret
place of the Most High
Shall remain stable and fixed
Under the shadow of the Almighty
(Ps.91:1)

ACT THREE

From Florida to Heaven ON EARTH

1956-1960

THE LOVE OF MY LIFE

I liked my job. Bessie was not only very pleasant she was a strong lady, a great worker and a friend. The two of us as a team were able to give good service to our customers and move our orders out quickly. There was a little space reserved close to the cash register where waitresses could sip coffee and just rest a minute. I always had a cup of coffee going and I liked to watch Michael as he expertly did his work. I found myself very attracted to him although he seemed to be totally unaware of me.

The hostess of the exquisite Chateau dining room was an elegant and nice looking single lady in her forties. She seemed very interested in our bachelor cashier too. I was only twenty-six years old and I think that she felt threatened by me. She became very hostile with me; later I realized that it was because she felt that this man was for her and not for me. It is true that Michael was forty-six and much closer to her age. I did my job well and was not compromising it in any way, so I ignored her many embarrassing comments. Underneath it all, a war was raging.

The busy winter season was in full swing; business was excellent and we were working seven nights a week serving gourmet dinners and Jewish specialties in this beautiful dining room with crystal chandeliers. There was not much time for foolishness and at the end of the day we were just tired and ready to go home.

My children's father had re-married now. She was a woman with four sons from a previous marriage and then she gave birth to a little girl. My children were now part of a large family; something I could not give them. I prayed to the God who healed my leg and led me to this country and He assured me that He was taking care of them; that was my only comfort.

We had worked three or four months steady now and although Michael was friendly, he made no other move. So at one point I wrote him a letter which I delivered in person. In it I told him that I would like to get to know him a little better but being that he was not asking me would it be rude of me to approach him? He answered the next day with a letter too and said he would be glad to meet me sometime for lunch. We started work at four-thirty now so that gave us a little spare time first. We set a date and place to meet. Michael drove us to the dining room of a nice hotel in Miami. It was quiet and comfortable and we had a very good lunch. We talked and became better acquainted. Then we decided that we would see each other again outside of working hours; this we did—a lot.

When the busy winter season slowed down, we took a day off and drove to the Keys to do some fishing. We left early in the morning and had breakfast there. Then we fished and Michael caught a large grouper. It was a beautiful fish and we took pictures. We put the fish on ice in the cooler and decided to drive back to Miami so we could eat the fish for supper. Michael drove to his mother's house and I was glad to meet this very nice Italian lady who I later called Mama Mia. We enjoyed our delicious fresh catch, but Michael was turning out to be the best catch of my life!

Michael had five brothers; four of them lived in Miami. Two of them were married. Michael took me to one of his married brother's house and we had lunch with them too. By the end of the working season (the dining room closed for the summer) I was well acquainted with his family, but most of all we enjoyed each other's company a lot.

By the time August rolled around it was getting more and more difficult to say "good-bye" every time he brought me home. He then told me that he was planning to spend the rest of his life with me. I knew that because of the age difference, he hesitated to say it, so I had to make the first move. I told him that I could not spend my life with him without being married. He jumped at the idea!!

MEET JACKIE CAPORASO

There was still a full month before the Chateau dining room re-opened. We had known each other for almost a year and we had no hesitation. I had fallen madly in love with this dear man who brought joy and peace to my heart. We decided to drive to New Orleans to get married, but when we arrived in Louisiana we found out that we could not get a license without my divorce papers and a blood test that required a three day waiting period.

I had not thought of bringing papers with me, and we really did not want to wait the three days for the test, so we just turned back and stopped in Mississippi. When we inquired at the Biloxi City Hall about a marriage license, we were told that we could get one right away for three dollars. Michael handed them a twenty dollar bill but the clerk did not have the change and it was about closing time. So I paid the three dollars for the license—the best three dollars I have ever spent!!

At the time, Biloxi on the Gulf Coast was just a beautiful strand of white sand beaches. There were no casinos and no gambling; just a very peaceful place. We drove to the town of Gulfport nearby and found the office of a Justice of the Peace who was glad to perform our little marriage ceremony. Mr. Cox was his name, and his secretary was our witness. We were legally married; it was September 9, 1957.

Several years later the Lord married us in the Spirit; He showed it to me in a dream, and as time went on, our walk together in the Lord was proof positive that this marriage was sealed in heaven. Michael and I were in perfect harmony, body, soul and spirit; a very precious blessing indeed.

Looking back on how things dove-tailed and took place in my life,

MICHAEL AND JACKIE

my heart leaps within me and I cannot help but know that it was God who worked out all these things for me. He had chosen Bill, my first husband, to bring me to this country and to give me two beautiful children. It was because of the hardships and heartbreaks of my life that he caused me to become seasoned enough to be a help meet to Michael. One may have thought that the first was a mistake, but on the contrary, all was very much a part of the chain of events that was needed for me to fulfill my calling in this life. Our God is amazing and He is no respecter of persons; He does the same for all if we recognize it.

I now had a new name and a brand new life ahead of me with a man I trusted and respected; I was very much in love. For the very first time in my entire life I felt safe, protected, and very happy too. I knew that together we would find the solution to any of life's problems that could arise.

PREPARING TO GO BACK

It was 1958 and Michael and I had been married about seven months when we decided that we should take a trip to France to visit my family. It had been twelve years since I left France and so many things had changed in my life. In January we booked a stateroom on the SS United States. We would sail from New York City on June 5th. The working winter season in South Florida is over after Easter and so it was a good time to take off. We had time to make our preparations. We would land in Le Havre and take the train to Paris to visit my father and his wife Georgette first. Then we would travel by train to Ghent in Belgium and see my mother, Armand her husband, and my brother Jean-Pierre who was now thirteen years old. I was very excited at the thought of seeing them all.

By mid-May, we had made all the arrangements for our trip on the SS United States. At the time it was the fastest ship afloat and it did not disappoint; we made the crossing in four days. We found a man who was looking for someone to drive his car to New York City. He was flying up but needed a driver to get his car there. It was just the right timing for us. He paid the gas plus ten dollars and we had the transportation we needed to get there with all our luggage. We did not have to worry about where to leave our car; it was ideal. We left a few days early to give ourselves plenty of time; we wanted to stay the entire summer in Europe.

I had written to my uncle Joe who lived in New York City. He was part of my grandmother's family from Alsace Lorraine but had immigrated to the States years ago. My mother had told me to make sure and try to see him when we passed by New York. She loved him and told me that they were about the same age and had been raised together. We looked him up and had lunch with him. He brought a gift for my mother and came to see us off on the ship. Michael and I dubbed him, "Uncle Joe."

MUST YOU GO PAPA?

It was in the night of May 26th that I awoke shaken by a dream. In the dream *I was looking at television when I see my father escorted by two men (one on each arm). They were all dressed in black. They approached the front of the screen and my father said to me (in French) "I have come to say good-bye!" I looked at him very saddened and said "Must you leave Papa?" He simply said "Yes." With that they all three turned around and started walking away. I kept my eyes on the screen until I could not see him anymore. That was the dream.*

A day or two later I received the telegram. My father had suddenly passed away. He had been in the hospital for some benign surgery and was ready to be discharged. But then, he got up to go to the bathroom and fell to the floor; it was a blood clot to the heart. He was gone that fast.

I knew that he wanted to see me again as much as I had wanted to see him. So he came to say good-bye the only way he could, through a dream. I was very grieved. It was May 28th 1958 and we were leaving for New York in just a few days; we would miss seeing him. I never forgot that dream although at the time I still did not connect it to God. Later, I realized that this had been a life-changing event for me.

Michael and I arrived in Paris and went to see my father's wife Georgette. Then we visited my father's new grave. Georgette seemed very cold. She could not even find a picture of my father for me. We left Paris quickly and took a train to Belgium to see my mother. Things were very cheerful there. We were warmly greeted by my now thirteen-year-old brother Jean-Pierre. My mother was ecstatic to see us. Armand came home from work that evening and mother had prepared a feast. It was wonderful and they loved Michael. The 1958 World's Fair Expo was in full force in Brussels and so we went with Jean-Pierre who was our happy host and guide. We had a wonderful visit.

Jean-Pierre had a beautiful choir boy's voice and he loved to sing. As a little boy he had sung "Holy Night" as a solo in the Cathedral in Ghent for Christmas. Now he was serenading us with a song like "Bridge on the River Kwai," in French of course. He was such a thoughtful young boy for all of his thirteen years. I had not seen my mother for twelve years and she must have been very excited about our visit because Jean-Pierre had lined the hallway of the house with pillows in case she fainted and fell when she saw us! She laughed about that but she really appreciated the loving care of her young son. Jean-Pierre would prove his love for her all along his short life; I loved him dearly too. More about Jean-Pierre later but for now back home again in Florida!

After our visit in Belgium we took a train to Switzerland and Italy. We went to the little mountain town near Naples where Michael's parents were both born and raised. We went to Genoa to find my aunt Angele. One of her three sons answered the door and said she was not available. She must have thought that I came to contest the inheritance that my father had left for her sons. That was not even in my thoughts. From Italy we went back to Paris and took the train to Aulnay to spend a few days with my Memere. She was so happy to see us. From there we took the train back to Le Havre to get on the SS United States and back home.

Later in 1964 and in 1972 we took trips to visit my family in France and Belgium only this time we drove and camped in our van through Holland, Belgium, Switzerland, Germany, Italy, Southern and Central France, Spain and Portugal. Michael was a wonderful driver and I was the navigator. Our little dog Teddy was a great traveler too; and he was the best guard dog for our van!!

AN EASTER SURPRISE

When we first were married, Michael and I agreed that we would never discuss politics or religion; we felt that those were hot button topics that could generate discord between us; we wanted to avoid that. So when at Easter of 1959, the desire to go attend Easter services began to stir within me, I was not sure how I was going to break the news to my husband. We had been married about a year and a half and life with Michael was just wonderful. I certainly did not want to spoil that.

Because Bill and his family were Methodist, when I first came to this country I had joined the Methodist Church; so I considered myself a Methodist. Michael had never been a member of any church. His family background was Roman Catholic but he had never been part of it. There were eight children in his family and none had been baptized as babies usually are in Italian families.

Michael was the third oldest of six boys and a girl; another girl had died as a toddler. When the oldest boy was about twelve years old, their father decided that they should all be baptized. When asked, Michael flatly refused and the father did not force him. Michael told me that he used to sneak out to a Protestant Sunday School and liked it a lot. So when his father wanted him to be baptized in the Catholic Church, he just declined.

I had no idea how Michael would feel about my desire to go to Church for Easter, so I went ahead and bought an adorable little hat with a wispy veil down to the nose. I showed him my hat and he was amused and laughed, *"Where are you going with this on?"* he asked. It really looked cute. I told him that I would like to go to the Methodist Church for the Easter services. I knew that they had a beautiful choir and nice music and I really would enjoy that. To my surprise he agreed to take me.

There was a large Methodist Church not far from our house so on Easter Sunday we dressed the part and went to church. The place was packed and people were standing in the front lobby waiting to be seated. We stood there as the ushers were going back and forth trying to find seats for the people. To our surprise one usher pointed to us and told us to follow him. He took us all the way down to the front row where there were two seats right on the front pew. Wow! There we were seated almost under the pulpit. The choir was fabulous! The music just moved something right inside of my being but that was not all.

At one point a lady soloist came to the front and we were asked to stand while she sang in an angelic voice "The Holy City." *"Last night I lay asleeping…There came a dream so fair…I stood in old Jerusalem beside the temple there…"* She continued with her beautiful voice and I listened astutely to the words. Somehow it was as if the Lord was speaking directly to my heart and revealing something that I had once known but had forgotten. Then she sang the last verse and tears began to roll down my face under the little veil of my cute hat. *"the light of God was on its street, the gates were open wide, and all who would might enter and no one was denied…"* The music was deafening and the crescendo was at its peak; my emotions were taking me flying in space and I was in a world by myself with…God.

I was not acquainted with the verses of the Bible; I had never read the Book, but somehow I knew that the Holy City in the song was not the actual place over in the land Israel; it had to be more than that. It was moving my entire being, and I knew that it was a place close to the heart of God. And it was a place that beckoned to me and that I must someday go to. I was a basket case.

Good thing that it was a long program; I had time to gather myself together again and it seems that Michael had not noticed my experience; perhaps he had been absorbed in his own, he never said, but from that day forward things were changing in our lives.

MY SECRET CRISIS

It was not long after that Easter that I began to feel as if I had fallen into a black hole. I had always been a cheerful and resilient person. It took a lot to get me down. But now I felt something strange happening within me, and I had no control over it. I said nothing to anyone as I did not want to admit to it, but I was very fearful of what I was feeling.

It was as though I was a small grain of sand lost in a vast universe all by myself. It felt like I had lost my foothold, and I was sliding down a slippery slope into a deep black hole. My entire being seemed to be pulled into a downward spiral. Questions were being raised in my mind, "Who am I?"- "What am I doing in this vast universe?" As time went by, this strange feeling swept over me more often, until I became truly concerned thinking that I may soon need help; perhaps a psychiatrist?

Should I tell Michael? He would worry and how could he help me? How could I even explain this to anyone? Then the thought came to me to kneel down and pray. I did and suddenly I knew that the same God who had once saved my leg would certainly hear me again. The answer came in a most unexpected manner.

Michael and I were both working. I worked with Bessie at a very fashionable steak house; I was a very busy person. But one day as I stood on the first rung of a little ladder in my utility room, I literally fell on my knees. Only this time it was not in prayer, it was an accident. My knees hit the concrete floor very hard and my left knee in particular was very painful. Michael's mother came out of her kitchen (we had a duplex and she lived in the front part with two of her sons while Michael and I occupied the back apartment.

Mama Mia, as I called her, helped me up and I limped into her kitchen where I sat on a chair. She brought some ice to put on my knee but it did not seem to help much. I was dressed ready for work and should be leaving now or I would be late. I made my way to the car and drove off to work.

I had been at work about an hour when my knee and entire leg was turning blue. It became so painful that I could not walk. Michael was at work but his brother Duke was at home with his mother. I called him and he came. He drove me to the emergency room where after a long wait and several x-rays it was determined that I had cracked my knee cap. It would take about six weeks of immobilizing the leg to heal.

When Michael came home that night he found me on the sofa with my leg in a cast, and crutches to clumsily move around. I had no idea that this was going to be God's answer to my desperate prayer. He put an end to my busy-ness and now He was about to get my attention...

Michael bought a portable toaster-oven and we set it up on the kitchen table (this was January of 1960 and there were no microwaves at that time!). With my little oven I could do a little cooking for myself while Michael ate at the hotel where he worked.

A week or two later, Pat Sawyer, a kind neighbor, came to visit. She had heard about my fall and brought me a nice lunch on a tray with a little bouquet of flowers from her garden. She also brought a book; it was a Bible. Pat was very pleasant and smiled a lot as she spoke softly. I thanked her for the lunch and the lovely flowers and she asked me if I had ever read the Bible. I did not want to sound stupid so I lied and said yes. She left the book with me anyway.

Because I told Pat that I had read the Bible, I felt that I had better try to read as much of it as I could so if she wanted to talk about it I would not sound so dumb. I randomly opened to the Gospel of Luke. I read that God cares so much about the lilies that He displayed them in beautiful attire. He also takes care of every sparrow, and how much more does He care about us and about me! I took each word personally, and then I read that God had counted every hair on my head and knew everything about me. I also read that of my own efforts I could not even add one inch to my stature.

As I read, something in me broke. These words were the answer to my prayer concerning the black hole that I had slipped into. As I lay flat on my back on my sofa, I felt that something was happening to me. I was being filled with a sense of joy that I had never known before. I was truly having a life-changing moment. Soon I realized that the "black-hole" that I feared so much was no longer there!

Over time, my good neighbor Pat kept bringing me lunch and then she announced to me that her Church (Christian Missionary Alliance) was going to host a Dr. Cox for their vacation Bible school. He was going to teach a series on the book of Hebrews. She invited me and I accepted. She said that she would set me up on the front row so that I could elevate my leg on a chair, and of course she would drive.

It was at the very first session on Hebrews chapter one that the heavens simply opened to me. I suddenly understood perfectly well that Jesus is the Son of God and that *"He was made lower than the angels for the suffering of death, that He by the grace of God might taste death for everyone.* (including me.)" (Heb.2: 9) The understanding came like something that I had known all along but somehow had forgotten.

I knew then that Jesus is the One who took away my black hole and set me free from the fear of losing my mind. My life was totally changed from that day forward. Jesus was real now and I knew that it had been His voice that I heard in my heart the night that I stood fretfully on the ship coming into New York Harbor– I just knew.

My knee cap was healing well and I was able to return to work only to fall again and fracture my pelvis. After that I knew that the Lord wanted me to change work. I took the job of cashier at the same restaurant, but then I heard that at the Florida State Employment Service I could take an IQ and aptitude test for a better job. Even though I had not been schooled in this country and had been trained with the metric system, I passed the test with a high score. So I was given the choice of several jobs. I took one as an assistant librarian for the Miami News; I liked it very much.

MY NEW PAL AND SISTER

My neighbor Pat, who had brought me lunch everyday when I had my broken knee, had become my best friend. She was like the sister I had never had. We got along so well on every aspect and I loved her dearly. She was the one who introduced me to church, to the Bible and to the reality of Jesus Christ in my life.

Michael and I attended Pat's Christian Missionary Alliance Church for a while, but then we found an Independent church called "Community Church" and we liked the pastor. He was a tall thin man very amiable and he taught from the Bible. It was in that Church that both Michael and I had our "born again" experience. We were happy to be members and we became serious Bible toting Christians.

One day there was a visiting missionary from Indonesia visiting at Pat's church. She invited him to dinner at her house and invited us too. The man was really different. He spoke about the baptism in the Holy Spirit and about the power of the Holy Ghost to heal and even raise the dead. He held our interest.

He was going to be speaking in a Pentecostal Church the following week and he invited us to come. His name was Brother Chung. One night, the Lord gave me a dream about him. I forgot what the dream was, but I do remember that it had to do with me giving him a pumpkin pie. When I saw him I told him the dream and he smiled. He said he never eats pie, except pumpkin pie.. He was impressed, and whatever the rest of the dream meant to him, he made note of it.

On the last night of his meetings there was a baptismal service. I had only been sprinkled in the Catholic and the Methodist Church, so he thought that I should be immersed; this was my opportunity. It turned out to be my first introduction to Pentecostalism! There was going to be much more to come as God was about to change Michael and my life again.

One day Pat told me that she had heard about a preacher in South Miami who was having meetings in someone's living room. She asked me if I would care to go with her. She explained that this man had been a Baptist preacher but was now laying hands on people so that they received the baptism in the Holy Spirit and spoke in tongues. This sounded rather scary to me but I trusted her judgment and figured that I could always walk out if I felt to. Michael was working that day, so I went with Pat.

When we arrived, the meeting was already in progress. The large living room was filled to capacity and all the people were standing while the preacher man was in front singing and playing his guitar. It was quite lively which was something new for me and I am sure for Pat too. We found two empty chairs in the back of the room and laid our Bibles on them; we remained standing with the rest of the crowd. Then the preacher began to move from one person to the other laying his hand on their heads and praying for them to receive the baptism in the Holy Spirit. I thought if he comes near me, I will run out; but he never did.

We sat down and he began to preach. He was very interesting and explained so that it was easy to understand. The teaching was rather lengthy but we made it through, and when it was over we did not linger. We had a long ride home and we both had to get back. This was my first encounter with the man called Sam Fife.

GOOD BYE COMMUNITY CHURCH

It had been a long time since I had had a dream of significance but I was about to enter a season when there would be many such dreams. These were so vivid and spoke so strongly that they could not be ignored or denied; most of all they came to pass. The first dream that made a lasting impression on me was the dream of the high bridge. *"I was standing by a swift moving river. Over the river was a very high bridge and a couple of professional dancers were dancing on the bridge. At one point the woman's ring slid off her fingers and fell into the swift waters below. They stood looking down at the water below; then the man dove in and swam all over the area looking for the ring, but he came up empty handed.*

At that same time I was standing by the edge of the water with other people by me. As it can be done only in dreams, I made an apple pie and retrieved it from the waters as if it had been fresh baked from an oven. I then took the pie and held it up to offer it to the couple on the bridge. It was then that they became very angry, even furious at me for having made the pie." End of dream.

Interpretation– The river represents the river of life that flows in the earth. The couple on the bridge is the church who is called to span the gap between God and man. Because they have become as professional entertainers to the people, the church has lost her union with the Spirit of God (ring). No matter how much they try to retrieve it, they are not able. However there are some in low places by the river of life who are able to retrieve the Word of God (a word fitly spoken is as apples of gold in pictures of silver Prov. 25:11) ready and appealing for the people to eat (apple pie). When the true word is offered to those who are in high places, they feel threatened and become very angry. They reject the Word and come against those who offer it to them.

Not long after I had that dream, we experienced the same anger against us that I had felt in the dream. Michael and I were still attending the Community Church we liked so much, so we thought it would be good to share the dream with our pastor. He met us in his office and we told him the dream. It was hard for us to accept what took place next. The usually warm and friendly face was twisted with anger and animosity. His lips trembled as he asked for our letter of resignation.

We told him that we did not want to resign, we really liked our church. He showed us the door and we went home. The next few Sundays, the pastor's message was filled with innuendoes and barbs like "the enemy in our midst," while he looked directly at us from the pulpit. We could not believe that this nice man had turned so hostile against us. We understood it was time to leave. We never wrote a letter of resignation, we just never went back.

God had closed that door, but another door was opening before us. Part of the dream had come to pass, but it would be repeated many times in our lives. Actually, in retrospect, we knew that the dream was our introduction to the call that the Lord had placed on our lives. After leaving the church we were joined to a group of like-minded believers and happily stayed with them for several years.

But then it happened again, the Lord spoke to our hearts and confirmed it through dreams, so that we knew that we had to present the word to the man in charge of the group. Each time, we found that the Word was rejected and sooner than later we were squeezed out of the group. This became a pattern until finally, we found no more groups to join.

OUR SECOND TRIP TO MAMAN

In 1964 we decided to return to Europe and visit my mother, stepfather and brother in Belgium. We also wanted to visit my Memere who was still in her little house near Paris. I had written to my mother about my new-found love of Jesus Christ and she quickly wrote to let me know that she did not want me to come to preach to her. I answered that she needed not be afraid. I wanted to keep the peace.

By now Jean-Pierre was eighteen years old, no longer the young boy we knew on our last visit. He was tall and extremely good looking with his stunning blue eyes. He was in college now and soon he would be working on a degree in philology (the study of languages). He would pursue it all the way to a PhD on the subject. His passion was to teach languages.

JEAN-PIERRE

We enjoyed him a lot on that visit. We had our van and our little dog with us so we added Jean-Pierre and his small motorcycle to the cargo and went to see my Memere near Paris. From there we took Memere and all went to Alsace to visit the family there! What a trip! It was great through the mountainous area of eastern France.

Our grandmother had not visited Alsace for many years and she was thrilled to go. It was almost dark when we arrived in Meyenheim and we were tired, but we found ourselves at the table in a rather animated conversation. Everyone was in a wonderful light mood and we laughed easily. The cousins were very happy to see us and welcomed us with open arms and a full table. They were humble farmers with an orchard of cherries and plums. With that combination they also made “kirsch,” a smooth liqueur that one sips with a lump of sugar.

The cousins spoke only German as they do in Alsace. Of course Michael spoke only English and I spoke French and English. Along with French and English, Jean-Pierre understood a good deal of German.

To go with the delicious home cooked food, the cousins kept pouring their delicious smooth white wine in our glasses and made sure we had ample supply of Kirsch too. Michael and I were not drinkers so it did not take much to keep us happy. The cousins spoke German and my grandmother translated it in French. I translated it in English for Michael. Sometimes, Jean-Pierre would try his German or his English too but mostly the room was filled with joy, love, and lots of laughter. The evening was a success and we all went to bed for a night of sound sleep. Early the next morning, we were awakened by the loud “cockerico” of an Alsatian rooster not far from our bedroom. Animals speak the language of their country as we do. The American or English roosters shout “Cockedoodledo,” but the French roosters come out with “Cockerico.”

OUR SHAGGY WORLD TRAVELER

After our short visit to Alsace, my grandmother took the bus back to Aulnay and Jean-Pierre rode his motorcycle back home. We traveled through Germany, Austria, Italy and Spain in our van, accompanied by our faithful and cheerful little dog. Teddy was a genuine Shnoodle (half Schnauzer and half Poodle). He traveled well and loved it. He was king of the road and king of the high seas too.

Many things happened to Teddy aboard ship, some funny and some not so funny, but he took them all in his good natured stride. He was a great pet. We bought him for ten dollars when he was just a small puppy. We had gone to see this breeder of poodles and while we were sitting in her living room inspecting the latest litter, this little shaggy puppy with hair over his eyes, brought us a shoe while wagging his whole body. He seemed to say hello, you finally came to get me! We knew he was our dog. His mother was a full blooded poodle who had an illicit affair with the schnauzer next door; thus our little Shnoodle was born.

In the different countries of Europe, Teddy learned the language. In Italy he quickly picked up on "Va Via" (go away) when we shooed other dogs away from him. When we said Va Via, Teddy looked around to see where the dog was and he would bark with excitement.

In Germany, it was "Gooten hound" (not sure of spelling but Teddy knew that it was talking about him.) He also knew that "fleish" meant meat when the butcher or the deli vendor spoke of fleish he perked up. It was in Germany that Teddy learned to go to sleep with "shlippen shloppen." From now on that was his command to lie down. Michael and I even used it to say good night to each other!! Our Teddy lived to a good old age of fifteen years. Then we had to send him to dog heaven. We buried him in our backyard here.

FOREVER YOUNG JEAN-PIERRE

Jean-Pierre was born on September 23rd 1945. He grew up to be very handsome and intelligent. He studied hard and earned a doctorate in philology which is the study of languages. He spoke Flemish, Dutch, German, French and Italian fluently. He spoke also Russian but not as fluently. We saw Jean-Pierre again on two subsequent visits. On our last visit with him, in 1972, he was married to Bernadette, a lovely young archeologist from Ghent.

Bernadette and Jean-Pierre spent their summers traveling to Morocco or Iran to do "digs" for her archeology studies. They were very much in love and well suited for each other; they were ready for the good life. Jean-Pierre had achieved the position of his dreams as a professor of languages at the prestigious University of Antwerp. He had worked hard for this, and at the age of twenty-nine he was reaping the sweet fruit of his labor. Alas, he would never get older than that.

It was in December of 1973 that I awoke one morning having had a dream that shook me to the core. I had dreamt that Jean-Pierre had suddenly died. I even wrote my mother about it but we both chalked it off quickly as just a dream!

However, in April of 1974 I received a letter literally bathed with tears from my mother. It was Easter vacation and Jean-Pierre, who had never been sick in his life, had cramps and discomfort in his stomach. It got so bad that he went to a doctor who prescribed some antacids. This still did not help so he went to the emergency room where they decided to operate right away and take his appendix out. That should have been the end of it, but a day or so later when the tests came back from the lab; they diagnosed him with an aggressive form of leukemia. My mother stayed by his side day and night, but on the forth day after his surgery, Jean-Pierre's heart gave up and he died; it happened that quickly! All his students came to his funeral and wept. My mother was inconsolable.

AU REVOIR MAMAN

Just before my birthday in February of 1977, my mother sent me a birthday card. In it were instructions of where to find papers and things in case of her death. I did not suspect anything because now that my brother was no longer there I figured that she was depending on me to attend to these things. However, it was only a few days later that I received an upsetting telegram from Bernadette, my brother's widow. It stated that my mother had suffered a massive heart attack on February 14th and they had found her dead in her apartment on February 17th. I knew that Valentine's Day was a very special day for her and Jean-Pierre. As I found out later, she chose that day to go and join him.

They kept my mother in the morgue so I asked Bernadette to make arrangements for her funeral. Bernadette was very obliging. I would pay the bill when I got there. After her husband's death in the late sixties, my mother had moved to Blankenberge where she loved to walk on the pleasant boardwalk; she had been very happy there. Now she had to be transported back to Ghent and be buried in the grave next to Jean-Pierre.

BLANKENBERGE BELGIUM

February 1977

Michael and I began to make plans to go as soon as possible. We needed a passport but we found that the one we had was still valid for three more weeks. Surely it would not take longer than that to get my mother's affairs in order. As it turned out Anita, my daughter who was in the Army at the time had received her orders to report to one of the Army bases in Germany (may have been Ramstein). She was driving down to see us before reporting in Norfolk VA for her flight over. She had made plans to stop and visit friends on the way down and I had no way of knowing where she was to notify her of the death; there were no cell phones at the time. Besides I really wanted to see her before she left for Germany.

A week later we flew to NewYork's JFK airport and caught our non-stop flight to Brussels on Belgium's Sabina Airlines. It was the very same night that Anita was flying over to Germany, only on different airplanes. We arrived in Brussels early morning and the porters and airport employees were on strike. So we sat in the plane for a while before they brought out steps for us to get off the plane. We walked to the airport and things were very quiet. Bernadette was there to greet us and drive us the distance to Blankenberge.

When we arrived, we first had to go to the police station to get the key to my mother's apartment. It had been sealed by law, and no one had entered since her death. This is the Flemish part of Belgium, so Bernadette asked us to sit and wait while she talked to the officers in Flemish. At one point one of them looked toward us and I clearly understood him to say, *"Is this the suicide case?"* At that, Bernadette said *"Shhh..."* trying to let them know that we had not been told. But the cat was out of the bag and I put all things together. My mother's birthday card and instructions of where things were to be found, and the fact that she died on Valentine's Day; it all fit. As it turned out they had found her prescription bottle opened and empty on the table. She had fallen on the floor after taking the entire prescription; it was lethal.

A couple of days after we arrived, a good friend of my mother came by to see us. Her name was Judith and she spoke English, French and

Flemish. She told us about her visit with my mother on the night before the incident. Mother had fixed herself a nice dinner of roasted chicken and peas. She told Judith that this was her last meal. Judith thought she just meant that she had really treated herself royally. My mother was a very jovial person who always cheered everyone, so Judith never thought that this was her plan. She took us all by surprise.

When after three days, the neighbors noticed that she had not been out at all; they became concerned and reported it to the police. My mother took a lot of trips and so it would have been normal for them to think she had gone to Spain or to some favorite winter spot. But this time, she had not mentioned going anywhere, and somehow they were suspicious that something was wrong.

The police came and were able to enter with a pass key. She was lying on the floor, it was February 17th but she had been dead for three days. On Valentine Day she yearned to be with her son and so she did it the only way she knew. When we entered, the place was a mess. The police had looked into everything to make sure there had been no foul play. The electricity had been turned off and the food was left to rot in the refrigerator. We had a job on our hands. We started cleaning right away because we had no other place to stay and the hotels were extremely expensive. God was with us, and He was about to show us His love in a way that we never thought possible.

ANOTHER CHAPTER IN MY LIFE

An entirely new chapter was about to begin in my life. We thought that we would be settling my mother's affairs very quickly, but we ended up staying in Belgium for almost two months. The rent was paid until March and the apartment was very comfortable; we stayed there. How the Lord went ahead of us in the events that followed was truly amazing.

We were located within walking distance of downtown where we could do our shopping. We could also walk to the railroad station which we would need to do a few times to shuttle from Blankenberge to Bruges to Brussels to Paris on cold and wintry February mornings.

The telephone was still turned on and we tried to call my cousins in Paris. We could not get a line so we called the operator. He would only speak Flemish and was no help to us. One must understand that there are two parts to Belgium. One is Flemish and speaks a language similar to Dutch or German. The other part of the country speaks French. There is a lot of resentment between the two, and the Flemish often refuse to speak French because the Wallones (French speaking Belgians) usually do not bother to learn Flemish. However, most of the Flemish speak French and also English.

At the same time, many Flemish resent the English who come over on holidays from nearby England to gamble in Blankenberge's casino. They are often noisy, get intoxicated and become offensive and rude. So the rather strait-laced and well-mannered Flemish people have a hard time tolerating them. When I tried to explain to the Flemish operator in French that I could not get a line to Paris, he thought that I was a Walloon, and when I spoke English, he may have thought that I was one of those English tourists. At any rate I could not speak Flemish and he would not budge.

The clincher came when Michael who was sitting near me said, "This is so stupid!" The man understood the word stupid and thought we had insulted him. Upon this he proceeded to disconnect our telephone and that was the end of that. From that time on we had to make our calls from a phone booth on the street. We found out later that a main telephone cable between there and Paris was down, and this was why we could not dial my cousins. The Flemish operator could not convey this to me at the time. Michael and I laughed many times remembering that out of all we said to this man to get our point across, he only caught one word "shtupid."

The next day, my mother's friend Judith came back to see us. We found out that she was a retired legal secretary and she spoke Flemish, French and English. She turned out to be indispensable to us; God had sent us an angel. Judith had the knowledge of law that we needed, and she could anticipate some of the legal pitfalls that we could encounter. She also knew the thinking of the area. More than that she became a trusted friend of ours; she was altogether a lovely person. We thanked the Lord many times for her. Judith was the friend and only person who had been with my mother on the evening before her death. In retrospect she realized that my mother had been planning her death for a long time.

THE ATTORNEY AND MY DREAM

The next order of things was to visit the attorney assigned to our case. He was assigned to us by reason of the district in which my mother lived. A few nights before our appointment with him, I had this dream. *"I dreamt that we walked in an office with a huge mahogany desk. Seated behind the desk was a large serpent. It was sitting up like a man and moving its head back and forth from side to side looking first to one side then to the other. There was something peculiar about this snake– When he opened his mouth I could see his molars!"* (Snakes have no teeth!)

At first I was not sure of the meaning of the dream, but on the day that we walked into the attorney's office, I had no doubt. The man seated behind a large mahogany desk politely bid us to come in and have a seat. He spoke fluent French as well as Flemish but no English. So I had to translate to Michael and that was good because it provided us with a pause to think things out.

We were just beginning our consultation when I noticed that this man had a habit of swaying his body back and forth and moving his head from side to side. My dream came vividly back to mind. The Lord had warned us; we were dealing with a slick and cunning character. What's more, the snake in my dream had molars, which meant that he could easily take a bite out of the money. This attorney was appointed to us by the courts so we had no choice, but in no way would we trust him.

As legal matters to close my mother's estate developed, we realized how truly blessed we were to have the very professional services of our friend Judith; my mother's best friend. She not only translated the language of the documents for us (all documents were in Flemish), but she also interpreted the law as it stood in that country. She had been a brilliant legal secretary and her experience was priceless to us.

To close my mother's estate I had to obtain what they called a "succession." The attorney explained the task ahead. Being that there was no will, I would have to prove that there were absolutely no other living heirs. Then we needed to pay all pending bills and debts.

An attorney would usually do this work which in this case could easily take a year of more. So we told him to let us know what he needed and we would do the "leg work," go to Paris ourselves and find the needed records. We also needed to go to Paris to close a savings account that she had told me about in her last letter. My mother had not left me any of the legal papers needed to get all this done and there were none to be found. It was not an easy task. If the Lord had not been with us to direct us, we could not have done it so quickly if at all. It was easy to prove that my mother's only son in Belgium was deceased, but I also needed to prove that she had no other children during her marriage to her first husband (my father). We would need an extract of her marriage certificate, which in France is called "livret de famille" or "family booklet. The birth of all children born during a marriage is recorded on that. I would also need a copy of their divorce decree, even one of her birth certificates.

Most of these should be on record in the Archives of the Hotel de Ville located in the center of Paris; that was our next task. While in Paris we would also get my mother's birth certificate; she was born in Paris. The closing of her French account would have to come last. As things developed day by day, we witnessed God making the way for us.

When we left Florida, our passport was only valid for three weeks. Time was running out, soon we would need to get to an American Embassy to renew it. There was an Embassy in Brussels but time was also of the essence so we first went to Paris to try to get the papers we needed.

MOTHER'S APARTMENT
And the Landlord

Although we were still comfortably settled at my mother's apartment, time would soon run out as the rent was only paid for two more weeks; we needed to liquidate the contents of the apartment. This was a huge job in a short time and so many other important things to do.

Blankenberge is a very nice resort town on the North Sea. It is situated close to the station of the hovercraft that goes back and forth to England across the Channel. It is very well known for its beach and boardwalk as well as for its gambling casino. So it is host to many tourists from England as well as from France, the Netherlands, Germany and many of the European countries in the area. Because it attracts so many tourists, everything is very expensive.

My mother's landlord came to see us. He was a very opulent and selfish individual who owned a considerable number of plush apartment buildings in Blankenberge. He pretended to speak only Flemish, so he brought a woman with him who could speak both French and Flemish. This lady was the overseer of all his buildings; she knew all his renters and was very valuable to him. He was a smooth businessman and had completed his education in the States. He was unaware that I knew this and I left it at that. I cannot remember his name but we will call him Mr. Shmartt.

Michael and I were aware that this man wanted everything for nothing. We had already talked about it between us and we had prayed. We knew that we were not in the best position to bargain so we had agreed that we would let Mr. Shmartt call the shots and the Lord would take care of us.

He spoke to Maggie in Flemish and she interpreted to me in French. In turn I interpreted to Michael in English. Mr. Shmartt was eager to buy my mother's furniture so that he could rent the apartment furnished and he was interested in getting a good deal.

My mother had been renting that apartment for over ten years, and all the furniture was hers. She also had a sewing machine and a beautiful set of gold trimmed Bavarian dinnerware. She had pots and pans, and good silverware as well as some very nice linens. She also had a mink coat and mink hat in pristine condition. My mother liked nice things.

The four of us were sitting at the large dining table and Mr. Shmartt began making offers for each piece of furniture and each item. He was shocked when Michael and I quickly accepted his offers without argument. We were totally at rest; we knew that the Lord was with us. Maggie was shocked at what was happening. She knew that he was taking advantage of us and she even tried to make gestures to help us, but what he was giving us covered the debts that we had to pay for my mother. It also covered her funeral expenses and the cost of our travels. He was really doing us a service because it would have been difficult for us to try and find a buyer so quickly, and be free to get back home as soon as possible.

Mr. Shmartt bought all the furniture, the dishes, the sewing machine, my mother's mink coat and mink hat, and he gave us cash on the line. This astonished Maggie. We explained to her about the Lord speaking to us and telling us to do it this way; she was impressed. She had been ashamed of the way Mr. Shmartt had taken advantage of our situation so she wanted to do something for us in return. She offered us one of her roomy and comfortable apartments free of charge for as long as needed when the rent ran out on this one. We knew this was also the Lord for us.

We only kept a few things such as the television set and small items that we had promised to give to Bernadette. She lived in Ghent so she came and picked them up later with her car. We also kept a few personal items that I wanted to bring home.

A couple of weeks later, when my mother's rent ran out, we moved into Maggie's comfortable and spacious apartment; the Lord's gift to us. Michael insisted on keeping the key to the mailbox at my mother's apartment for a while longer. This proved to be a very wise decision.

Note: A month after we came back to Florida, Maggie wrote that Mr. Shmartt had suddenly died of a heart attack. He was not an old man. The fear of the Lord came over her and she gave her life to Jesus Christ. This was a beautiful part of our trip.

SHUTTLING TO PARIS
Another angel

Our goal was to acquire the "succession" papers so that I could legally close my mother's accounts. It was bitter cold and windy in Blankenberge, but we walked very early in the morning to the Railroad Station to catch the train to Brussels where we would run to catch the one daily train to Paris.

In the last birthday card she sent me, my mother had told me, that she had an account in a certain Bank in Paris. We needed to look into that as well. We would have to make at least two trips to Paris. Each time, the Lord prepared the way for us. He posted His angels along our way. There was the time at the Brussels Railroad Station that we could not find the quay to our waiting train.

A gentleman in a felt hat ran behind us calling, *"This way, this way!"* He had been on the Brugges train with us and had recognized that we were Americans. Just before we boarded the train to Paris, he explained to us, with tears in his eyes, that after WW2 the Marshall plan that the U.S. had set up in Europe saved the lives of many people who had lost everything and were desperate. He had been one of those people and now he was so happy to have the opportunity to thank us. He was one of God's angels to us.

There was the time at the Rail Station in Paris when we stopped at a stand to get coffee. We laid our heavy briefcase containing our money and all our papers, on a bench. We walked away to catch our train when a man running behind us caught up with us. He was holding our briefcase; we had left it on the bench! This was unbelievable for us! This man had been watching us; he truly saved our life. Definitely one of God's angels.

While we were still at my mother's apartment, another one of her dear friends came to introduce herself to us; her name was Gabrielle (talk about angels!) She invited us to her house for dinner. The three of us had an angelic visit Michael, Angele (my real name) and Gabrielle, what could go wrong? As we left she handed us a key. Gabrielle had moved to Belgium years ago, but she had kept her apartment in Paris so that she could visit with family there. In memory of her friendship with my mother, she told us that we could stay there free of charge for as long as we needed. What a wonderful provision. Besides saving us a bundle of money, it became a God-sent for us when we needed to prove residence in Paris. It was a residential address, not a hotel! Gabrielle was truly an angel of God for us.

GOD'S AMAZING TIMING

Gabrielle's one bedroom apartment in Paris was the most comfortable little nest anyone would ever want to stay in. It had a very nice bed, a kitchen well equipped with pots and pans and everything one needs to cook dinner. It was cold in Paris in February-March but the little place was warm and cozy. On the street floor of the building there was a butcher shop on one side, and a bakery on the other side. The baker fired up his oven at about four in the morning and the delicious aroma of fresh baked breads and croissants filled our bedroom and whetted our appetites; it was delightful. The butcher turned out to be a great help to us as you will see.

We went to the archives of the Hotel de Ville in the center of Paris and found records of my mother and father's marriage certificate and divorce decree. We had copies made of these. We also went to the 8th district where my mother was born and obtained a copy of her birth certificate. However these documents could not be handed over to us. It is the law in France that such documents, when ordered, be mailed to the address of residence. It was good that we had kept the key to the mailbox at my mother's apartment in Blankenberge. We had those papers sent to that address.

NO COINCIDENCES

In the meantime, three weeks had gone by and our passport was expiring very soon. In order to renew it, we would have to go to an American Embassy. We thought we would go to the one in Brussels, but it was while we were delayed in Paris that our passport expired. So we went to the American Embassy in Paris and that was also the timing of the Lord!

We had not anticipated having to stay this long in Europe so we did not bring personal papers such as birth and marriage certificates; all needed to renew a passport. Being that we traveled with a passport I did not bring my citizenship papers either. At the Embassy, they gave us forms to fill out. Michael's parents were not born in the U.S. and he could not answer much concerning them. I did not even know the ID number of my citizenship papers. We filled out the form to the best of our ability. We were amazed when one hour later, we walked out of the Embassy with our beautiful new passport in hand. Note: At the time, a married couple could travel together with only one U.S. passport.

Most important still, this new passport listed our address of residence as the little apartment that belonged to Gabrielle. Later, we realized how impossible it would have been for us to orchestrate all these events so that we could close my mother's account. The Lord had surely gone ahead of us.

THE PARIS BANK ACCOUNT

In her last correspondence with me, my mother had given me some details concerning a small bank account she had in Paris. So we went to the Bank in question and I made my request and showed my mother's death certificate. They wanted to see my identification and I showed them our passport. They asked, "Where did you get this passport?" I answered, "At the American Embassy here in Paris." They noted that the address on our passport was not of a hotel; it was a residence in Paris. This was proof for them that we lived there and that we were not just tourists. There was a law at the time that French money could not be taken out of France!!! The fact that we had to renew our passport in Paris was not mere chance; it was our Father's well prepared plan for us. He is so good!

That was not the end of this episode, because the bank did not release the money that easily. They told us that we would receive a notice from them at our home address (Gabrielle's apartment). We would need to bring the notice to the bank to collect the money. This was their way of making sure that we were the right people.

BLESS THE BUTCHER

The butcher played a valuable role in the success of our task in Paris. Because we had a kitchen I was able to cook our suppers and I had bought some of his nice meat on several occasions. He was a friendly person and he knew us by name already. What happened next could have never planned in advance. Obviously, our Father had gone before us and set the stage. We were expecting the important notice from the bank by mail, but now realized that we had no mailbox in the building. And what was even worse, the postman did not know us and had never heard about us! Where would he deliver this mail? And what day would this mail arrive?

Actually we had not even given it much thought until one morning when we were on our way out. We were already a few blocks down the street when it dawned on me that the notice may come that day. We walked back and I felt to ask the butcher if he would mind taking any mail that may come for us that day. His shop was opened and it was possible that the postman ask him if he knew us.

When we came home that afternoon, we checked with the butcher and sure enough he had our notice. This is what happened. The regular postman was sick that day and the substitute was not acquainted with the names of the people in the building. When he did not find a Caporaso mail box, he asked the butcher about it. The rest is history. Someone was doing the thinking for us and certainly looked out for us that day!

We took the notice to the bank, collected the money, and closed my mother's account. But now we had to return to Belgium and take the money with us. It was not a whole lot, yet it was enough to keep us going in Europe.

The next hurdle was to take the money back to Belgium with us. At the time it was the law in France that no French money could be taken out of France. So Michael put the money in his money belt and we took the train back to Brussels. When the train passed the border between France and Belgium, the custom's agents came on board to check our passport; first the French agents, then the Belgian. We were asked by the French if we had anything to declare and we quickly answered no. That was that, we had passed the border and taken the money out.

The next step was to exchange our French francs into Belgian and American currency. Again this was not a problem because Blankenberge is a casino town year around. This meant that the banks had exchanges facilities to make it easier for the tourists to buy Belgian francs (this was before the Euro). Even though we were not gambling, we were able to change our money with no questions asked.

We knew that the Hand of the Lord was upon us; He touched everything we had to do. He had seen fit to let our passport expire in Paris so that we would have proof that we were living in Paris. He had seen fit to put it on the heart of Gabrielle to loan us her apartment so we had a residential address. He had seen fit to let the postman have the flu on the day that our bank notice came. He had seen fit to let us talk to the butcher so that he took the mail for us. He had seen fit to let us go through customs with no problem.

He had seen fit to let us keep the key to my mother's mailbox so we could receive our papers from France. He had seen fit to move on the heart of the woman who let us use her comfortable and beautiful apartment just for the cost of utilities. And was it by chance that my mother lived in a casino town so we could easily exchange our French francs? Someone may say these were all coincidences, but we know that our Father and Lord was answering our prayers and meeting our needs with a high Hand.

MR. LAWYER SHOWS HIS MOLARS

Our lawyer could not believe how quickly we were moving this case; we were working hard and wasting no time. We needed to go home. We had been in Belgium since February 24th and on March 25th, which happened to be my mother's birthday, I received the final papers of my "succession." Now I could inherit her Belgian account and close all the loose ends and return home to Florida. There were still a few bonds invested but they could not be cashed for several more months until they reached maturity. We left those in the hands of the attorney.

We made our arrangements to return home. We thanked dear Maggie for her goodness to us. We paid her for the utilities, and her husband drove us with all our luggage to the airport in Brussels; we paid him for that. It was now the end of March and we had been gone longer than planned, but the Lord had shown us so much love!

BACK HOME IN FLORIDA

We were back home and it was July when the bonds that the lawyer had been holding for us, matured. I wrote to him and received no answer. Finally he sent a note with some excuse that he could not legally cash the bonds and that he would have to re-invest them for us. He asked for a fee to do that. At that point I remembered my dream of the snake with the molars. This man was looking for ways to take a bite out of our money. He had told us at first that it would take about two years to close our case, but because we had done all the leg work, it had taken a little less than six weeks. He had not made the money he wanted to make on us. So now he was looking for ways to make a little more. We realized that this had turned into spiritual warfare.

HAPPY TO BE BACK IN FLORIDA

It was then that the Lord handed us some solid advice. I felt to ask my deceased brother's wife, Bernadette to help us. As it turned out this was another of God's "coincidences." Her father was a prominent judge in the affairs of Belgium. Would he be willing to put pressure on this attorney and make him do right? Bernadette helped us and asked her father for us. I could just imagine how surprised our snaky lawyer must have been when he was contacted by this judge in high places! He released the funds right away. At that time I needed a lot of dental work and we also needed a new vehicle; the bonds took care of all these things and we were very grateful.

If we learned anything from this experience it was that our heavenly Father is very interested in all the small details of our lives. It is not by means of big miracles that we learn to walk in faith. It is as we see Him in every little detail that He so lovingly brings to our daily lives. There is no way of life that compares to this daily walk with Him. This is far more rewarding than a religion; it is abundant life.

And I will give them one heart
A new heart
sensitive and responsive to their God.
(Ezekiel 11:19)

ACT FOUR

DANCING WITH THE KING

1979-2004

LADY PASTOR?
OH NO!

I titled Act four "Dancing with the king" because of a dream that I had about that time. In the natural I have never been a good dancer, but in the dream I was just flowing with the Lord and enjoying it so much that it was hard for me to wake up. He then let me know that He was going to teach me how to stay in perfect step with His Spirit and enjoy it.

Many were the times that I felt a twinge of fear thinking that the Lord would ask me to do something that I just could not do. I found out that He never asked me to do anything that He had not prepared me for. And I found great joy and delight in His upholding arms, as He led every step of the way.

When we settled back home from Europe, I remembered the promise that I had made to the Lord when we first got to Belgium and faced such a gruesome task. Michael and I both re-dedicated our lives to Him and waited for Him to move. It was not long until it came in a way that we least expected.

Dottie was a neighbor living with her mother a few blocks away from our house. She was a like-minded believer and Michael and I would sometimes stop by her house when we took our evening walks. One evening while we were visiting, Dottie asked if we had heard a certain preacher by the name of Jake Townley on the radio. She said the program was called, "Voice of the Layman."

She explained that Mr.Townley is from Candler which is a community about seven miles north of where we live. She insisted that it would be good for us to call them because what he had to say sounded just like the things that we often talked about. When we left, I told Michael that this man was probably very nice, but more than likely he must be another Baptist preacher; this area is strongly Baptist. I had no desire to follow up on this.

To my surprise, Michael brought the subject up again later that night. He said that it would not hurt to call and find out if they met anywhere and perhaps we could visit at least once with them. We looked them up in the phone book and found a number.

The next day was Monday and Michael called. He spoke with a lady named Helen and found out that she was the wife of this radio preacher Jake Townley. She told Michael that indeed they met in a church building in Candler every Monday night. Michael decided that we should go. My heart was not in it, but I did not argue as I saw his determination.

We found the church. It was a nice size building, but that night only a hand full of people was present. The teacher was not Jake Townley. It was a young man that they called "Chofskey." He was teaching from the Bible but he seemed to fumble a lot over the meaning of the Scriptures that he had chosen. At one point he asked if anyone could add to what he was saying and I found myself speaking up with what I felt was the answer. The people looked at me, and I noticed that the lady sitting near me was making note of my name written in gold letters on the cover of my Bible that lay on the chair next to me.

After the meeting, we introduced ourselves and told them how we had heard about Mr. Townley. They were happy to meet us. It was obvious that they were hungry for the Word, but their young teacher did not have much to give them. We went home and did not mention that night again. It was about six on the following Monday evening that our phone rang and a lady named Cleo was on the line.

She was from the little group at Candler. She was the one who had taken my name down from my Bible cover. She evidently had found our number in the phone book and decided to call. She asked if we had planned on coming to the meeting. Before I could answer (we had not planned on it) she quickly said that Chofskey had called and could not come to teach them that night.

Then she dropped the bomb—could I come and teach them instead? I had not taught for several years. I had no idea where they were spiritually and I had nothing prepared. We needed to shower and dress and be there at seven!! I was about to find a way out when I heard the Lord saying, "A servant of the Lord must be ready to teach at all times." I had told Him that I would do whatever He said; it was time to obey. I told this lady that we would be there.

The people were few but they hung on every word as one would delight in fresh baked bread. Michael and I went back the following few Mondays and listened to their usual teacher. We could feel his resentment building toward us. At that time, the Lord gave me a dream and showed me that I was going to be their next teacher…I said nothing and just waited for the Lord to move.

We attended their Monday night meetings for several more weeks but we could sense that the people were not satisfied with their teacher. Then one day, Cleo, who was the grandmother of the Townley children, approached me. She told me that all her grandchildren needed to be taught, and she asked if I would open a Sunday school for them on Sunday mornings. The nice church building was available and Mr. Townley took care of all the utilities and upkeep. Michael and I prayed and talked about it. We agreed that we would take it on a trial basis.

The first Sunday morning, I came prepared to teach children with a flannel board and cut out figures. However the seats were being filled with the parents who brought their children to school; they all stayed. So I was teaching the children and the parents at the same time; this continued for several Sundays.

Then Cleo approached me again and said that she would teach the little children in separate rooms and I could teach the parents and teenagers. Little by little this children's Sunday school became family Sunday school and Church on Sunday morning. Michael and I were sure that some of my teaching would not be accepted, and that all this would not last more than three months. But they loved the Word and loved us. We loved them dearly as well and they treated us like family. All together we taught in the church for sixteen years.

It was during those years that our old friends Phil and Jane came to visit at our house. They mentioned their friends Ernest and Nancy Brown from nearby Ocala and thought that we should meet them. Phil called them and gave me and Michael the phone. Soon after we met

Ernest and Nancy, and from that day forward we became very close friends. They came to the Candler church and Ernest taught too, confirming the Word.

We closed the teachings at the church in 1996. The Lord let us know that our time in Candler was fulfilled. One Sunday morning, I announced it to the people. Some wept; they did not want us to go. But when God closes a door, it is closed. Candler was very special to Michael and me. The Lord had given me a shepherd's heart for the people and I loved them dearly. I still see some of them occasionally, but 1997 was a year of serious changes in my life.

In 1997 Jake Townley fell ill to lung cancer and soon went to be with the Lord. It was a sad day for all; God had called him to the other side of the veil. It was that same year that I began noticing subtle changes in my dear Michael. He was a fighter and would not give up easily but one day he said, *"Whatever happens I want you to know that I never mean to hurt you."* He knew that he was slowly losing his memory and that he was not always in control of his actions. At times he would cry and sometimes he would run away and I could not find him. For the first time in my life, I was really afraid.

During the following three years Michael went through difficult times as his mind was being distorted by dementia. He was denying the problem and I was in denial myself. He did not want to seek medical help; I felt trapped. Michael had a medical discharge from his time of service and so he had VA medical privileges. One day, he agreed that he should go to a VA doctor. We went to Gainesville, a town 55 miles north of our house. As it turned out, this particular VA hospital is joined to Shands Teaching Hospital and has many young doctors finishing their internship before going into practice. At the time, they were conducting studies on the effect of Alzheimer and dementia in older men, the Lord had made the way.

Michael's first doctor was a young doctor from Philadelphia who was almost finished with his internship; his specialty was psychiatry. It did not take him long to diagnose the problem and to know what to do to help. He put Michael on a medication and told him that from now on he could no longer drive. Michael never put up any resistance, and from that day forward I did all the driving. Once, as he sat next to me in our little car he looked at me and said, *"You are a very good driver and I trust you."* This made me feel so good. I knew that he was reaching out to me with so much love. He was placing himself in my hands.

During the following four years the two of us went through many good days and some very dark moments. Michael was so depressed at times that he could just break down in unstoppable sobs at the drop of a pin. He knew that he had lost his identity and he just could not take hold of it again, but he was trying so hard. Michael was a fighter and he would not give up easily.

Michael could no longer express his love for me as he desired, and as he was so good at doing, but I saw it in the many little things that he did and that he tried to convey. He could always pray and loved to be told that Jesus loved him; his spirit was alive and well. But the strong man that was guarding the house had taken dominion over his body and had managed to scramble his brain. Yet in spirit and soul Michael remained a beautiful person.

TIME TO SAY GOOD BYE

One may think that God only speaks through pious and religious words and deeds, but I have found it to be much to the contrary. God often uses popular songs and events to speak to His people. God is not "religious," He is "holy."

The Lord speaks in many ways. So many times He has spoken to me through ordinary love songs or popular songs. I remember when I dreamt that I was behind a pulpit singing one of Edith Piaf's favorite songs.

Edith Piaf was a typical Parisian singer, very famous and much loved. With great passion, she sang those French love songs that tear at your heart. One of her very popular song is called *"La vie en rose."* Literally translated the title means, "Life through rose colored glasses or life in the pink." In the dream, I remembered every word as I was singing it in French to the people of the Candler church.

The words translated in English are, *"When He takes me in His arms and speaks to me softly, I see life in the pink. He tells me words of love, words for every day, and it does something to me. He has entered in my heart, He speaks to me of happiness of which I know the source. It's Him for me, me for Him, for life, He has told me, gave His word to me for life. And as soon as He appears, I feel my heart beat faster within me."*

Through the dream, this song was no longer a Paris street song; it was a love song from the bride's heart to the Lover of her soul. The Lord was going to give me words that would reach the heart of the people and let them express their true love for Him. The French words conveyed the response that He desired from their hearts. He wanted to hear it. Soon after, the Spirit began to give me teachings that opened their hearts to His love. Just as the words of the song conveyed, they responded to His love.

One night in 2003, I had this dream, *"I was in the bathroom and saw traces of blood on Michael's towel. I knew that he was bleeding from the rectum and that the source of the bleeding was from very high up. I also knew that Michael was very tired and would soon go to his rest."* I told myself that the dream had a spiritual meaning and that the Lord would soon make it clear. Michael had recently completed his physical exam; he had passed all the tests with flying colors. I watched to see if blood was ever on his towels or garments, but I found nothing, so I forgot about it.

It was in the spring of 2004 that the Lord spoke to me through another song. This time it was not in a dream, it came as I was mopping my kitchen floor. One of my favorite songs was playing but for some reason the words caught my attention. The song was called "Time to say Goodbye." I had heard it before, but that morning the words moved me to tears and I heard the Lord saying in my Spirit, "This is especially for you."

I did not want to hear what my heart was trying to tell me. But the song kept on playing and the words kept on ringing in my heart. I began to cry as I pushed the mop; it was a moment I will always remember.

Michael's physical health was just fine. However his mind was worsening and on his last visit to the doctor, in July of 2004, I was asked to start looking for a nursing home for him. I had already made inquiries, but my heart was not in that. I knew that as long as he was not violent to himself or to me, I would be able to take care of him at home. I had asked the Lord, "How long will I be able to endure?" The Father spoke directly to my heart, *"You will endure to the end."* Whatever that meant, I believed Him and found peace.

It was the last weekend of July when Michael complained about one of his legs hurting. I looked and saw a strange rash on the back of the thigh and on his back end. I thought it may be shingles so I called the VA hospital in Gainesville and spoke with a nurse. It was Saturday and his doctor was not there but the nurse assured me that they would send me some cortisone cream and that it was not shingles. He said that shingles usually did not appear on the legs. So I was more relaxed about it and began treating him with some of the cortisone cream I had on hand.

Michael was not a complainer but he did mention several times that his leg was hurting. I gave him Tylenol and it seemed to help him. However on Monday, I decided to make an appointment with a local dermatologist who confirmed my fears—Michael had shingles. The doctor prescribed a very strong medication that would help quickly and it really did. Within two days the shingles were still very visible but were nicely drying up.

The prescription was to be taken for several days; however after three days I noticed that Michael was extremely pale. His appetite was good, he did not seem to be feeling bad, but one afternoon while we were in the backyard, I saw him get so pale and sweaty that I ran to him. He was passing out. I sat him down in the grass and gave him water. He said he was better. He stood up, walked into the house and went to bed. Later, he got up and ate supper, but he remained very pale.

The next day, I called the dermatologist's office and inquired about the medication. I felt that perhaps it had been too strong and was causing a reaction. The doctor gave word through the nurse to take him off the medication; however he suggested seeing his family doctor because he did not feel the medication was really the cause of his trouble. The next morning was Thursday. I made an appointment with a local doctor; however he could not see him until the following Monday.

The next day was Friday and we were going to do a little grocery shopping. We were both ready and went out to the car. Michael was trying to open the car door when I noticed him getting very pale again. I ran to him and held him; he was again passing out. I walked him back in the house and he went to bed. I asked him if he felt to go to the hospital, but he emphatically said NO. I knew that he would fight me if I insisted so I just let him go to bed. I thought that it would take a few days for the strong medication to be out of his system and he would be fine again.

It was early Saturday morning and I was sound asleep. I had not been sleeping well these last few days, and months and years for that matter, but that morning I was sleeping so well that I did not hear Michael get up. I awoke suddenly and saw that the lights were on in the kitchen. I hurried and got up. Michael had shaved. This was so unusual these days because as a rule I would have to insist on him shaving. But that morning, as if he had somewhere to go, he had shaved.

He came into the kitchen and I looked at him. He was pale as a sheet and ready to topple over. I ran and caught him and sat him down on the kitchen chair. He was gasping for air. I ran to get the phone and came back to hold him. I first called my neighbor so I would have someone to help me, then I dialed 911 and asked for an ambulance.

My neighbor came in and it was not long until the ambulance with the emergency team was here too. Michael had rallied a little and was trying to walk but they put him on the stretcher and took him to the emergency room.

As the doctor examined Michael, he quickly found fresh blood from the rectum. It did not take the doctor long to diagnose that Michael was bleeding internally. He needed a transfusion right away so he was admitted to the hospital. They would have to give him a colonoscopy and an endoscopy to determine the source of the bleeding. My thoughts went back to the dream of the previous year; my heart was pounding.

The next day was Sunday when he had the endoscopy. The bleeding did not come from his stomach. That evening a few friends came and we gathered around Michael's bed for prayer. Michael prayed too; he loved to pray. Our friend Willie began to weep. He had a vision of Michael; it was too beautiful to describe. He saw him in such a place of beauty and peace that it was too much for words. Willie was overwhelmed. He stayed with Michael that night so I could go home and rest.

On Monday they took him for the colonoscopy.

AN UNEXPECTED VISITOR

In the afternoon, I was sitting alone in the room with Michael when a nurse in a crisp white uniform with a little winged white starched hat on her head entered the room like a gust of wind. She was very blond with ringlet curls cascading down the back of her head. She was not dressed like the other nurses, but she seemed to know what she came after. She walked quickly to where I was then back out. On her way out she turned to me and pointed her finger. With an intense look in her eyes, she locked into my eyes and said, *"You can stop it, you know!"* I replied, *"Stop what?"* She said, *"The colonoscopy."* With that she wafted out of the room as if carried on a breeze.

I thought, *"How strange! She knows it is too late to call off the colonoscopy. Besides, the doctor has no other way to find the source of the bleeding and stop it. So I could not really stop it now."*

After the colonoscopy I was informed that Michael had no cancer, but they still could not pinpoint the source of the bleeding. I would have to wait for the doctor to come in. That morning as I was sitting by Michael's bed, I heard the voice of my heavenly Father in my heart. He asked me, *"What do you want me to do?"* I said, *"Father, you know my heart, and you know all things."*

The colonoscopy had been very hard on Michael. He never fully recovered from it, and they still did not find the source of the bleeding. Because of his mental condition, he was required to have someone with him at all times. There were no nurses available to do this. I was thinking of paying someone I knew to come and sit while I went home to rest a little and get something to eat. But the Lord had other plans to provide for me.

Terry, a dear brother in the Lord came from forty miles away and stayed another full night. My dearest friend Nancy treated me royally. She came each day all the way from Ocala and brought delicious food and snacks. I will forever be grateful to all of them. My Father had it all arranged for me.

It was Tuesday morning. Nancy and I were sitting in the room when the doctor came in. He quickly announced that Michael was bleeding pretty fast now. He needed another transfusion (his fourth). He also said that he was going to prepare him for another colonoscopy. It was clear that a vein or artery had been ruptured in the upper part of the colon and they had been unable to locate it the first time. It was then that I remembered the strange nurse that had pointed her finger at me. I told the doctor that I did not feel Michael could stand another colonoscopy.

Then I questioned the doctor, *"Supposing you find the source of the bleeding, then what do you do?"* The doctor came closer to my chair. He looked at me and said, *"Actually, there is not much we can do. He is not a candidate for colon surgery. There is another procedure that we can do but that does not usually work and if it does it is only temporary."* At that point I knew that the blond nurse had been sent from the Lord. I told the doctor that I did not want him to have another colonoscopy. I wanted to take him home.

It was then that the doctor came over to my chair and looked me straight in the eyes. He said, *"Not many women have the strength to make such a decision but it is the right thing to do. Whatever you do, don't ever feel guilty for this and know that you still have a purpose for your life."* He then left the room and came back just a few minutes later to say, *"If this was my father, I would do exactly the same."* My friend Nancy was sitting there at the time.

After that, things moved very fast. Michael was quickly slipping into a coma. I had kissed him and told him that I was taking him home. I promised him that no one would ever hurt him again. It was then that he opened his eyes. They were clearer than I had ever seen them. They were beautiful eyes filled with all the love that he could find in his heart for me. He said, *"You have pretty hair."* These would be his last words to me.

By Tuesday afternoon, hospice came to take over Michael's care. I told them that I wanted to take him home. Nancy was with me and was again a great help and comfort to me. I had to go home to open the house for hospice. They were bringing a hospital bed and many other things that were needful for his care. There would be a prescription for pain medication too. So I left and Nancy stayed with Michael. He was in a light coma now, and we were hoping that he would stay with us until he was back home. This had been his desire. The service that hospice gave us was outstanding; early that Tuesday evening, Michael and I were home.

It seemed that Michael knew he was home. As soon as he entered the house, his face relaxed and he was at peace. I took off the tight elastic stockings that they had put on his legs and he sighed with content. I knew that even in a coma, he had a sense of awareness. One of my good neighbors went to the drugstore and filled his prescription for me. Another brought food and drinks. The Lord continued to take care of us.

THE FINAL HOURS

I have wished many times that I could have that time to live over. I don't think that I realized how close the end really was. Michael was very quiet, he was in a coma but I figured that he was resting well now. I was sleepy so I went to bed but slept only lightly. The Lord told me that He would awaken me if needed. During the night Michael began to breathe heavily and noisily. I knew that this may be what is called the "death rattle," so I prayed that the Lord would take that away. He did, and Michael began to breathe easily; the rattling noise was gone.

At eight in the morning a nurse from hospice came. She gave Michael a nice dry shampoo and washed him. She took his temperature and it was 105, extremely high. I turned the air conditioner higher and we prayed that the fever would drop. It went down to 102. Anita called from Newark airport. She was on her way here and would arrive early afternoon. Would she see him alive?

At ten o'clock the hospice nurse and I were standing by the bed. I looked at Michael...He was very peaceful as if in a deep sleep, but then I noticed...he had quit breathing. The nurse took his blood pressure...there was none. He was gone. So easily, so quietly, so softly, he just slipped away like the gentleman that he always was...my love had moved to the other side of the veil. It was August 11th 2004. I began to pace the floor. The nurse said that I could call the funeral home when I was ready. I waited about an hour. I said, *"I will not rush you out of your house..."* But finally I called and they came. I hated the way they took him in the back of a van...I wished I would have called a different funeral home...I wanted him to be treated with so much dignity...Yet, Michael was no longer in that body...He was gone in a much better place. Later, he showed it to me.

At the same time that all this happened, hurricane Charley was in the Gulf of Mexico barreling down on Florida. The funeral home waited to set the date for the funeral as they were not sure where it would make land. I prayed that it would stay south of us; it did. It was a devastating hurricane that hit just below Tampa. The funerals were set for August 15th.

Michael was buried in the little Candler cemetery surrounded by others that he loved. As Michael had wished, there was only a graveside service. Our dear friend Ernest Brown officiated. Anita and Nancy stayed close to my side. So many loving friends came to say good bye and pay their respect to this wonderful man. The entire Townley family and their children came and family in the Lord from the Citra group. Neighbors came and also sent food and money. Many sent cards. Dear friends supported me with their love and financial help. I felt surrounded by the arms of the Lord Himself. I will forever be grateful.

Anita stayed an entire week. It was so good to have her with me. There were many legal papers to take care of, and things can get blurry at times like these. Anita helped me think and keep on track; she was a pillar for me. All that week we ate the delicious meals that friends had brought; that was a Godsend. The love of God shown through His people overwhelmed me. Thank you Father.

When I found myself alone again, I found the strength of the Christ within; I felt secure and safe. I wrote in my journal, *"The Lord is so close and my Father is so real. Michael's love did not leave me; I feel surrounded with love."*

POWERFUL MESSAGES FROM ABOVE

As I am writing this today, it has been almost four years since Michael left; time has gone so fast. I fared well, yet many waves of grief passed over me for most of the first two years. And today, it still seems as if it all happened yesterday; the memory remains vivid.

A few powerful occurrences need to be mentioned. The first of these took place exactly one month after Michael left. It was seven in the morning on September 11, 2004. I was in bed sound asleep. I recorded the incident in my journal, *"From a sound sleep I heard Michael's sweet voice. It was loud and clear and sounded young, happy and peaceful; it was so nice to hear. He said 'Good Morning!' as he had so many times in the past. It was so real that it woke me up. I felt very comforted."* I had prayed that the Lord would show me how Michael was now. I know that this was the Lord permitting him to assure me that he was very happy and peaceful. That was the first of several such encounters.

On December16, 2004, I dreamt that *"I was in a large Walgreens. I had a prescription to fill for myself. I handed it to the clerk and was told that it would take about an hour before it was ready. I said, 'Good, I will just go to dinner.' Then I started looking for Michael. The store had two sections and I spotted him with a buddy in the other section. He was so very happy. He had found this buddy and was the happiest I had ever seen him. I decided to go to eat by myself while waiting for my prescription."* When I awoke I knew that the Lord was telling me there was a prescribed healing for my grief. I only had to wait a little longer for it, and in the meantime I just needed to partake of His Word which is food for strength.

The dream also showed me the joy that Michael is sharing with His Buddy (the Lord Himself). Michael has found the Christ in all those who are together with him behind the veil.

It was on my next birthday in February that I asked the Lord, *"When will I get my prescription for healing?"* He answered, *"NOW!"* With that, I felt joy flooding my entire being. I knew I was healed from grieving.

A little later on August 30, 2005, while dreaming *"I saw Michael sitting on a very comfortable chair in our bedroom. He was dressed in his favorite wide striped blue and light grey sport suit with sky blue pants.* (We always thought he looked like Jacques Cousteau in that suit) *He looked so clean and radiant, like he had been scrubbed. I knew he was ready to go."* The sky blue pants denote that Michael is walking in heavenly places.

What I dreamt on September 28, 2005 was so real that I was not sure I had really been asleep. In that dream *"Michael was lying next to me in the bed. I held unto his arm very tight and asked him if he knew just how much I loved him. I knew we were no longer into things in the flesh. He said he had come to help me and give me pointers on how to do the things I needed to do."*

Then I awoke and had to go to the bathroom. I reached with my hand for Michael next to me but he was no longer there. I thought he was in the bathroom so I waited until I could no longer wait. I took a peek into the bathroom and saw that he was not there. It was then that I remembered that Michael was no longer here, and realized it had been a dream. This dream was a special blessing because after that, I noticed that when I had to do things that were a "man's job", like checking the air in the tires or nailing down something that had come loose, I found the ability to do it.

And then there came a time when I felt guilty for Michael's death. I had been told that this often happened to those who lose a loved one. Somehow the enemy is able to tell them they could have done something to save their lives. I did not think this would happen to me, but it did.

Then on February 12, 2006, this dream came as a birthday present to me, *"I got up and went into the kitchen. At that moment Michael walked in from the utility room, just as he had the morning he passed out and I called 911. However, Michael was now a tall and vibrant young man. When I approached him I thought that he snubbed me because he did not say a word. Instead, he scooped me up into his now strong arms and held my head gently against his chest. He told me he loved me and that I had nothing to be ashamed of; I had done nothing wrong."* What a relief this was for me! I was free.

These times of visitations from Michael comforted me for two and a half years. But on November 5, 2006, things were about to change again. I dreamt that *"I had fallen into a deep dark narrow place like a manhole. I was climbing out of it through a rope ladder that was against the wall. It was very wobbly and difficult, but now I was on the last top rung of the ladder and I would need to pull myself up the rest of the way with my arms. However I was still too far to reach up to the top. I knew I could never pull myself up that far.*

It seemed that I had been in the same predicament before, but then Michael had been standing at the top and had pulled me up by the arm. So now I was calling Michael from the top of my voice, but I knew that he could not hear me because he had now moved to another room. Then a man appeared by the hole. He was very kind and extremely strong. I asked him if he would help me. With one strong hand he took hold of my arm and pulled me up and out." (End of dream)

When I awoke I knew that the Lord was telling me that Michael, who had been close-by these many days, had now ascended higher and could no longer be here to help me. During our lives together, Michael had a way of pulling me up out of my "manholes" when I was down. At the time of my dream, I had been feeling a little down. So the Lord was telling me that I could no longer depend on Michael to pull me up. Now I could fully rely on the strong Arm of the Lord Himself!

Thank you Father for teaching me this lesson, and for your great help in my everyday life. Thank you for showing me a little of the life that goes on beyond the veil. You also made me know that after passing from this life, one is allowed to stay around to comfort and help those who are left behind. My life has been and is beautiful from beginning to end...and there is no end...it goes on into eternity.

EPILOGUE

After Michael left, I lived alone for over four years, but I was never lonely. I learned to take care of the house by myself and I have been absorbed in my writings. My children and my extended family in Christ are a great joy and support to me. They are special blessings in my life and I shall never forget them. I can never thank my God enough for giving me Michael to share my life with and for revealing His Son Jesus Christ in me.

As I close this writing, my daughter Anita will soon retire and come to live with me. We will be happy and comfortable in this little Florida house that Michael built. I am looking forward to our times together. I have no doubt that each day will continue to be an experience of growth in the things that matter most.

Things of the past are only a preparation for the greater life that will forever unfold and expand before us.

With much love, ***Jackie Caporaso***